SELLING, START ASKING

THE MOST POWERFUL PSYCHOLOGICAL QUESTIONING TECHNIQUES TO BOOST YOUR SALES SUCCESS

ROMAN KMENTA

Imprint

1st edition 04/2023

Cover design: Monika Stern / sternloscreative
Layout: VoV media
Illustration: VoV media
Editing/proofreading: VoV media
Image copyright: Freepik hole-from-ball 73

Publisher: VoV media - www.voice-of-value.com

ISBN Paperback: 978-3-903845-54-1
ISBN Hardcover: 978-3-903845-55-8

TABLE OF CONTENTS

QUESTIONS - THE RUNGS ON THE LADDER TO SALES SUCCESS

The customer enters the barbecue store and asks for a charcoal barbecue model XY. The salesman shows him the appliance and is delighted. Finally, a customer who knows what he wants. The customer still asks for a discount, gets a discont, buys and pays. The salesman is happy. After all, he has made a profit, 550 euros at least. On closer inspection, however, there is no reason to rejoice. In fact, this is an almost traumatic experience for any real salesperson. A fat black day in the calendar. One that should make him seriously think about hanging up his job - better today than tomorrow ... Before the boss takes the decision away from him. Over the top, you think? Let's take a look at how this customer contact could have gone as an alternative.

Customer: *"Good afternoon, I would like to have XY charcoal grill."*

Salesman: *"Ah, the XY. A good device."* He saunters over to the device with the customer. *"May I ask you a few questions about it?"*

Customer: *"Yes, I'd be happy to."*

Seller: *"Is this your first grill?"*

Customer: *"No, I have an old charcoal grill that is disintegrating into its component parts."*

Salesman: *"I see. And what's your favorite thing to grill?"*

Customer: *"The usual. A few steaks or sometimes fish when guests come. Mostly on weekends."*

Salesman amazed, *"That means you don't barbecue during the week?"*

Customer: *"No, I usually work long hours and my wife is not a fan of building a fire. When I get home, it takes me too long to get the grill ready."*

Salesperson: *"But in principle, you wouldn't mind having a steak during the week?"*

Customer: *"No. But why do you ask?"*

Salesman: *"Well, I just mean, if there was a possibility to grill something in between in a hurry ... Would that be interesting for you?"*

Customer: *"Already."*

Salesperson: *"And what about when you have guests. How many is that usually?"*

Customer: *"That can be as many as six to eight people."*

Salesperson: *"That means you are well occupied with fire building and grilling and have little time for your guests?"*

Customer: *"Yes, unfortunately. I often don't get to talk until everyone has eaten."*

Salesman: *"It's a shame, though, isn't it? Wouldn't it be nice if you could devote yourself entirely to your guests?"*

Customer: *"That would be great, but unfortunately, it only works when my wife is cooking something. It's difficult when we're grilling."*

Salesperson: *"And if it could, what would you think?"*

Customer: *"That would be interesting, but what are you getting at?"*

Salesperson: *"Have you ever thought of using a gas grill?"* - Meanwhile, you are standing in front of a medium-sized gas grill.

Customer: *"Not really. I don't have any experience with that yet."*

Although I haven't provided a full transcript of the sales conversation, you can see where it's headed and how it's likely to end. With my extensive experience in grill sales, working with manufacturers and dealers in the industry for many years, it's probable that this customer will choose the gas grill for €1,450. If the salesman continues to do an excellent job, additional accessories worth a few hundred euros may be added to the sale. Compared to the first scenario, sales have tripled or quadrupled. What caused this increase? The salesperson had a different fundamental understanding of their profession and, in accordance with the theme of this book, focused on asking goal-oriented questions. As I will demonstrate throughout this book, the path to greater sales, increased revenue, and satisfied customers is paved with questions.

Why questions are important

Questions and questioning techniques often fail to excite participants in sales seminars. It appears too basic, even mundane. And, to some extent, it is. Asking questions is not a difficult task, and it may seem banal to some. However, as is often the case in both business and life, simple actions can have a significant impact. In communication and sales, few techniques have a more profound effect than asking the right questions at the right time.

Asking the right questions at the right point in the sales conversation will bring

- better customer relations,
- more new customers,
- more clarity about what customers want,
- higher attention from customers,
- fewer discounts and lower rebates,
- a higher completion rate,
- more revenue per customer,
- more additional sales,
- higher credibility and a stronger expert status (those who ask - technically - good questions show that they know their stuff),
- and, if something goes wrong, complaints with a happy ending.

There is hardly any area in the sales conversation or process in which questions do not play an important, even decisive role.

I have not yet mentioned one very important point:

"He who asks, leads!"

It is incredible how closely leadership in a conversation is linked to questions. The person who asks the questions holds the reins of the conversation. Often enough, I experience that this is the customer ... but generally, it should be the salesperson.

The image that many have of salespeople is that of someone who persuades others until they give up and buy (in the positive case). Not that there aren't salespeople like that, but they're usually not the most successful. They do this partly because they like to talk, and partly because they are so knowledgeable about the subject that they simply know a lot about the product and think that the customer needs to know all about it.

"Professional idiot talks customers to death!"

…is a fitting adage in the sales industry. However, true professionals in sales know that talking incessantly is not the key to success. Instead, the most effective salespeople ask a lot of questions and listen attentively. Listening may appear to be a simple, unremarkable skill, but it is anything but. In sales, attentive listening is essential to understanding customers' needs and desires, identifying their pain points, and ultimately closing deals.

And while asking questions and listening are so easy (they really are), they are the very skills that are rarely applied - in the sales seminar as well as in the wild.

And it is precisely this combination of an incredibly effective and versatile communication tool - questions - on the one hand, and the so weak skills of many salespeople to use them professionally on the other, that prompted me to write this book.

I can live very well with writing a book about something simple, maybe even banal, if it's something highly effective .... And I am convinced of that. Questions, the right questions in the right place, are the leverage that will not only make your sales conversations a little better, but catapult them to a whole new level. Let me surprise you.

Enjoy reading and good luck with the implementation!

PS: ... and perhaps you will notice while reading that some of the questioning techniques are neither quite so simple, and certainly not banal. Behind some of them there is even a lot of psychological depth - no wonder, since some of them come from coaching. At the latest, when you start using them in your sales conversations, you will realize that solid mastery of the questioning technique in a wide variety of sales situations is one of the more demanding tasks in sales.

What questions can be used for

The areas of application of questions in sales are manifold. There is hardly a subarea in the interaction between salesperson and customer in which questions do not play an important if not decisive role.

Specifically, in this book, we will look at the use of questions in the following areas of sales:

- Telephone appointment acquisition,
- Relationship building,
- First-time customer contact in retail,
- Needs assessment/needs analysis,
- Demand generation,
- Presentation,
- Objection Handling,
- Price negotiation,
- Graduation,
- Upselling,
- Cross-selling/additional sales,
- Customer loyalty,
- Complaints and grievances.

This book is entirely focused on sales and written for salespeople. All the examples of questions you will find in it will fit one of the sales situations listed above. However, you will find that you can use the same questioning techniques (sometimes just with different content) for many other areas in your life:

- Leadership of employees,
- Shopping,
- Child rearing,
- Initiate relationships,
- Leading relationships

- to name just a few of the more important areas outside of sales or customer contact in general.

How this book is structured

The book essentially consists of two main parts. In the first part of the book, you will find a variety of questioning techniques, which are listed alphabetically for convenience. This makes it easier for you to find or look them up. This first part is the foundation.

The second part is about the practical application of these questioning techniques in all the areas of application listed earlier. There you will find many examples of very specific questions that you can use 1:1 (if you wish) in your sales practice.

PART 1:

TYPES OF QUESTIONS

The types of questions in this section come from different areas. It is, if you will, a "best of" from coaching and sales practice. However, it would be wrong to think of coaching and sales practice as two separate application areas in terms of questions. The questions asked there and there are partly different in content, but structurally very often the same.

The question, *"What do you want to achieve?"* - a goal question - is one you can ask in exactly the same way in coaching as in sales. Why am I mentioning coaching at all? There are two reasons. First, people in coaching (across a wide variety of directions) have been quite intensely involved with questions and questioning techniques, and have produced so much useful stuff on the subject. Secondly, a well-conducted sales talk could also be called customer coaching - so similar is this in its basic structure and questioning technique to a coaching session.

The following list of questions does not claim to be exhaustive. There are several more. Sometimes the same type of question can be found in literature and practice under different names. This is what I have mentioned again and again.

One realization you will also have when dealing with the different types of questions is that they overlap. One and the same question often fits into different categories.

"What exactly do you want to achieve with this action?" is, for example, an open-ended question, a target question, a fact/information question, and a concretization question. This may sound a bit confusing at first. However, you can completely relax about this. In the end, it's not about being able to assign each question exactly or knowing what each category is called. Rather, it's about having a variety of good questions at your fingertips so that you have the right one for every situation. What it is called is ultimately irrelevant. Only for the book and the explanation of the questioning techniques are the names and the division into different question types helpful.

And it is precisely this fuzziness in the assignment, the fact that one and the same question fits into different categories, that makes questioning techniques particularly exciting. This kind of combination creates entirely new, more multifaceted and often much better fitting questions.

"What will it be like when you reach your destination?" - relatively matter-of-fact question - can be much more productive when combined with an emotion-related question: *"How will you feel when you have achieved this?"* can elicit completely different reactions from the customer. In other words, combine and mix just the way you like it. The result is all that matters.

Now, before we get into the types of questions, we have to deal with one more thing that is so extremely important in the context of questions that it simply has to be at the beginning.

Listen professionally

The whole questioning technique is of no use to you if you cannot listen. Only by listening does a question become a question. Otherwise, it is just a conversational phrase that largely fizzles out without effect. Listening is at least as important for the successful application of questioning techniques in sales conversations as the questions themselves.

Now you might think that listening is not that difficult and that we do it all the time anyway. In my experience, we do it less and less. Even in everyday conversation situations, there are fewer and fewer people who are really good listeners. Perhaps this is due to our increasingly fast-paced time. Everything has to happen quickly. But really good listening needs one thing above all: time.

And even though we often don't think we have them, taking the time to listen in sales conversations is a very good investment. If you truly listen, it will result in your customers opening up to you much more, telling you much more (yes, sometimes things you don't want to hear), and talking more. That takes time. But here, quality clearly goes before quantity. It's better to ask a few questions and listen really well than to pester the customer with a battery of questions.

Real sales professionals can do both: ask lots of good questions AND listen very intently.

What listening brings

"Listening is what most people do. Listening is a skill that few have mastered."

Effective listening has been shown to have various psychologically studied effects and impacts. However, even without scientific studies, your intuition likely tells you the same thing. In sales, listening serves two essential purposes:

- **Emotional effect**
  Listening creates trust, builds or strengthens relationships and makes the listener likeable. In private life, too, good listeners are the ones you go to when you want to talk about a problem.

- **Factual effect**
  Listening provides information. This is the very basic function of listening. Listening well when answering a question often gives you the best ideas for what to ask next.

How does listening work

To distinguish good listening from normal hearing/ perceiving, the term "active listening" has become established for it. This designation emphasizes that listening is an active process. It requires doing something, not just passively receiving information.

Essentially, you should pay attention to the following elements when "active listening" or incorporate the following "activities" when listening:

- **Keep eye contact**

- **Nod**
  This does not mean that you agree with what is being said. Rather, you are signaling to your customer that you are fully with them and listening.

- **Giving words of confirmation**
  Words like *"Aha", "I see"* or similar have the same effect as nodding.

- Even **sounds like**
  "*Mmmh*" or an audible exhale have the same effect as nodding. Everyone has experienced the other person on the phone asking, "Are you still there?" This is usually an indication that the confirmation sounds have been missed.

  To increase understanding of what has been said and to signal to the customer, "I'm listening to you," it is important to ask intermediate questions. These can be questions of concretization or often also feedback questions (more on the two types of question later).

- **Mirroring" your counterpart's body language**
  Mirroring your counterpart - simply put, adapting your own body language, specifically your own sitting position to that of the customer - is an extremely powerful tool. It is often mistakenly devalued as "mimicking." But rather, it is something we do all the time - and thus, something quite natural.

If you observe two people engaged in a good, intense conversation, you will observe exactly these elements in both of them. That is, they are already doing this in various situations anyway. However, I notice again and again that what we do as a matter of course in private conversations, completely without thinking about it and usually without even realizing it, is not done in sales conversations. These are sometimes much more "artificial" than conversations in private. This may be due to the - sometimes tense - situation that selling can sometimes be. Especially when it comes to a new customer or a particularly important conversation.

Therefore, as a professional salesperson (which you are, otherwise, you wouldn't pick up a book like this and certainly wouldn't read it), it makes a lot of sense to consciously engage in "active listening" as well.

It is best to consciously pay attention to this at the beginning of a conversation (you usually don't have any difficult topics to discuss then) in order to use it unconsciously later on.

Grammatical question types

Although I had announced that the question types would be arranged in alphabetically ascending order, I broke this rule right at the beginning. It remains the only, but important exception. If you look at questions from a very basic grammatical point of view, there are three categories that can be used in combination with all of the following question types. Therefore, I put them here at the beginning:

- unanswered questions,
- closed questions,

- alternative questions.

These three question types differ in terms of the set of answers that are possible in each case. All three types of questions are certainly well known to you, although you might have to think about them for a moment if I asked you to give me an example of each. But thinking briefly - for such basic types of questions - already seems to me to be far too long. As mentioned, from my point of view, the goal of professional salespeople should be to be able, at three o'clock in the morning, to shake suitable questions on any topic out of their sleeves. So let's delve deeper into all three categories. You'll see what treasures there are for you to discover.

The open questions

Open questions are so called because they leave the type and amount of answers open or - as one also hears from case to case - because these open up the counterpart. Both explanations make sense. *"What all do you need?"* is an example of an open-ended question. Open-ended questions are those that begin with question words (some are still preceded by a preface).

Examples of open-ended questions:

- **Like** - *"How are you?"*
- **Who** - *"Who is responsible for this in your company?"*
- **What** - *"What do you use to clean your dishes so far?"*

- **Where to** - *"Where should we deliver the products?"*
- **Which** - *"What dimensions should the wheels have?"*
- **For which** - *"Which of the variants did you choose?"*
- **How long** - *"How long will it take you to make a decision?"*
- **Since when** - *"Since when have you been using this lubricant?"*
- **Where** - *"Where do you want to use the product?"*
- **About what** - *"What are you about?"*
- **What for** - *"What exactly do you need the vehicle for?"*
- **Why/Why** - *"Why don't you buy from your current supplier?"*

By the way, these question words are an extremely good thought guide when it comes to thinking about what you might ask. Just use them as a guide and go through them one by one in relation to your product. You will probably quickly come up with a suitable question that starts with one of these question words.

Maybe you got stuck on the last question, the one with the why, because you once heard that people shouldn't ask why.

And yes, it's true that a direct and blunt why question "forces" the customer to justify themselves. Therefore, when asking such why questions, it can be helpful to work with justifications (more on this shortly). However, even if justification pressure is created by a why question, this does not mean that these questions are wrong or cannot be used in sales.

There is nothing that cannot be used in sales

At this point - because it is just fitting - a basic statement, a short digression that does not only apply to the use of questions: There is nothing in sales that is fundamentally wrong. The problem is not that we make mistakes in sales, or use wrong or bad techniques, such as why questions. The problem is not the techniques, strategies, or tactics. The problem is - and this is very common - that salespeople are not aware of what you are doing or saying and what they are accomplishing.

Yes, "why" as a question word - especially when combined with the appropriate tone of voice and body language to emphasize it - can create pressure to justify. But this is not fundamentally bad or wrong. If my strategy as a salesperson is to create pressure to justify a particular situation, then everything is fine so far. The goal is to do whatever I do as a salesperson quite deliberately and intentionally. So there may well be situations where, for example, creating pressure to justify myself in a conversation may be an appropriate course of action.

In sales, you have the freedom to pursue any approach, even those that contradict the principles outlined in my books, as long as you have carefully considered your strategy. Knowing what you are doing and understanding the potential outcomes of your approach are crucial components of success.

Wide or narrow opening angle

It makes sense to distinguish between open questions with a very wide opening angle and those with a rather narrow or even very narrow opening angle.

- **Wide opening angle:** *"How was your vacation?"* Just about anything can come as an answer to this question. Long stories or just a short *"nice"*.

- **Narrow angle of opening:** "*When will we see each other again?"*
  In principle, the answer to this is limited to dates and times. Of course, a client who has recognized the suggestion in the question (more on that later with suggestive questions) or simply doesn't want to see you could answer *"Not at all for now."*

When we talk about open-ended questions, we usually mean those with wide openings, although the others are also open-ended questions.

Open questions - when to use

The use of open questions results from their mode of action. What can this type of question do for you in the sales conversation? Open questions ...

- Provide a lot of information (especially those questions with a wide opening angle), because the set of answers is open.
- Contribute to the interlocutor opening up and telling more.
- Create or strengthen the relationship with the counterpart, because you have more opportunity for active listening due to the usually detailed answer of the interviewee.

Open-ended questions are particularly suitable for starting a sales conversation when you still know little and want to learn as much as possible. However, being able to answer open-ended questions presupposes that the customer is in the know. Let's say you ask a customer who has been watering his garden by hand, doesn't want to do that in the future, and is therefore interested in an irrigation system: *"What should it be able to* do, *the system?"* That in itself is a neat, open-ended needs assessment question. Nevertheless, you may only get an irritated questioning, *"Well, watering the lawn, I would have thought ...?" as* an answer, because he has not yet informed himself about the possibilities offered by irrigation systems nowadays. For such cases, you need other types of questions to get the relevant information - question types such as the next one.

The closed questions

Closed questions limit the answer options to yes or no. Theoretically, at least. You've probably seen a customer give a very long and comprehensive answer to a closed question like *"Should the tractor also have GPS connectivity so that it can be computer-controlled and automated?"* However, some also only answer with a simple yes or no. It depends a little on the conversation situation and the customer's conversational skills whether closed questions are also answered in a closed manner.

Closed questions - when to use

Closed questions are very suitable for the following areas of application:

- If you want to get the clearest answers possible.
- If (as in the irrigation system example) you want to ask about wants, needs, and requirements from a customer who has little idea of what they want to buy.
- If you want to slow down someone who likes to talk a lot and for a long time (with open-ended questions, you reinforce talking a lot).
- If you want to work through a list of items for which you need information in the form of a yes or no.
- If you want to make a customer's statement more concrete.

Often - but not necessarily - as mentioned, open questions tend to be found at the beginning of a sales conversation and closed ones later in the further course when it comes to clarifying individual points.

The alternative questions

A very exciting category of questions are alternative questions. These are those in which the answer alternatives are already given in the question. *"Do you want the sweater in green or blue?"* could be such a question with two answers. But you can also ask it with three alternatives: *"Do you want the sweater in green or blue, or will you take both colors right away?"*

Why is this a particularly exciting type of question? By specifying certain answers within the question, you influence the customer's answer - in many cases, even very massively.

An example to illustrate the point: As part of a study, guests at a hotel were asked at breakfast, *"Do you want a breakfast egg?"* - a closed question to elicit demand and at the same time to close the "sale" right away. Some guests said, *"Yes, please"* others *"No, thank you." There* were probably also a few who answered, *"Bring me two eggs right now please!"* even though the answer was not actually a choice. A count was made of how many breakfast eggs were sold that way.

In the second phase of the study, the nature of the question was changed. The new question was *"Do you want one or two breakfast eggs?"* - an alternative question. What do you think? Did the changed question sell more eggs? If you think yes (as probably all other readers do), you are correct. Significantly more were sold. Why? Because by prescribing certain answers, the guest's thinking was steered in new directions.

Of course, in the second phase, it would have been perfectly legitimate to answer, *"Thank you, but I don't want an egg."*

But the likelihood of this happening was significantly reduced by the fact that this alternative was not available for selection. Some of those who did not want an egg chose the "lesser of two evils" and took only one egg. Coming up with an alternative answer - no egg - and then saying so takes extra energy. At the same time, those who like eggs and were hungry probably chose the "two eggs" alternative very willingly. All in all, the sum of these choices leads to significant differences between variants 1 and 2. This a very good example of the communicative power inherent in alternative questions.

Strictly speaking; however, it is not only the given alternatives that play an important role in this example, but also suggestions in the form of presuppositions (pre-assumptions), which represent a very strong psychological lever. More about this is in the section on suggestive questions.

Alternative questions - when to use

In terms of areas of application, alternative questions are similar to closed questions. You should use them ...

- If you want to get the clearest possible answers.
- When (as in the irrigation system example) you want to ask for wishes, needs and requirements from a customer who has little idea of what he wants to buy.
- If you want to slow down someone who likes to talk a lot and for a long time (with open-ended questions you reinforce talking a lot).

- If you want to work through a list of items, each of which has two or more alternatives to choose from.
- If you want to concretize the statement of a customer.
- If you want to influence the customer's responses (as clearly shown in the breakfast eggs example) in a certain direction.

The influencing effect of the answer specifications and the presuppositions even goes so far that it is sometimes not at all easy to formulate a neutral alternative question - one that does not influence the customer as much as possible and does not steer the answer in a certain direction.

Amplifier for questions

There are various techniques that you can use - so-called amplifiers - to give your questions even more emphasis or to increase the likelihood that you will receive an honest answer to them. With these amplifiers, we can distinguish between

- verbal amplifiers,
- body language amplifiers and
- the silence as an amplifier

distinguish

Verbal reinforcers for questions

You can ask questions "stand alone" or also add something. The following additions to questions bring - depending on the question and situation - different advantages for you:

- Question Permission,
- Justifications,
- Information,
- Benefit arguments,
- Objection anticipation.

Let me explain all four additions in a little more detail.

Question permission

When asking a question, you ask your customer if you can ask them a question:

- *"Can I ask you a question?"*
- *"Can I ask you a few questions about that?"*
- *"Is it okay if I ask you a few questions?"*
- *"Would you answer one more question for me about that?"*

The question permission is typically formulated as a closed question, with the intention of eliciting a "yes" response. This answer need not be verbalized, however; it may be a tacit agreement or simply a lack of objection from the customer. Regardless, this technique increases the likelihood of a response, allowing you to proceed with further questioning without creating an awkward dynamic with the customer.

Justifications

In behavioral psychology studies, scientists have found that reasons for a wish, a demand or even a question increase the probability of getting what one wants - in the case of questions, an answer.

Examples of justifications

- Instead of, *"Can I ask you a few questions?"*
    - *"So I know exactly what you need, I'd like to ask you a few questions. Is that all right?"*
- Instead of, *"Do you want to try it?"*
    - *"Because it's much easier to make a decision when you've tried the product yourself, I want you to do just that. Is this a good fit for you?"*
- Instead of, *"Would you give me the order now?"*
    - *"So you can have the vehicle in time for your vacation, would you give me the order today?"*

Especially with sensitive topics, ones that your client may not be comfortable talking about or even talking about with everyone (money, health, sex, etc.), it is very helpful to add a rationale.

- *"In order for me to search for the right offer for you, I would still need to know roughly what your budget is for the apartment."* (A question that - strictly speaking - is formulated as a statement).
- *"In order to meet regulatory requirements, may I still know if you have been vaccinated or tested?"* (An alternative question frequently heard from restaurants during the COVID crisis).

Information

Information is particularly important when the customer still does not have enough knowledge to make a decision. This information must be combined with a question. The advantage of this approach is that the customer has to respond immediately by giving an answer instead of just being bombarded by information. As the salesperson, you can retain control of the conversation.

In sales talks, the mistake is often made that salespeople reel off a lot of information, but do not link this information to questions and thus do not really make progress in the sales talk.

Examples of information in questions:

- *"The window is available with double or triple glazing for extra sound insulation. Which variant do you want?"* (completion-oriented alternative question)
- *"The model comes in 190- or 230-horsepower variants. Which do you prefer?"* (Alternative question in the needs assessment)
- *"For 29 euros extra, you also have breakfast included. Do you want that?"* (Closed additional sales question)

As you can see, information can be added at various stages of the sales conversation. This type of questioning can be used particularly well in the needs assessment and presentation phases.

<u>*Benefit arguments*</u>

The transition between neutral information and benefit arguments is fluid. It is often quite easy to derive benefit arguments from information. In our previous examples, this could be something like this:

Examples of benefit arguments:

- *"The window is available with double or triple glazing for extra sound insulation. With triple glazing, you have the advantage of ensuring that you are not disturbed by passing cars and wake up in the morning completely relaxed and rested. And you said that you have problems with the previous windows in terms of noise. Which variant would you like?"* (Conclusion-oriented alternative question)

- *"The model is available in the 190-horsepower or the 270-horsepower version, if you want to treat yourself and have even more driving fun. Which do you prefer?"* (Alternative question in the needs assessment)

- *"For 29 euros extra, you also have breakfast included and save money, because breakfast costs 35 euros per person if you book it only on site. Do you want to book that right away?"* (Closed additional sales question)

It makes sense, of course, to add the benefit arguments to the points or variants you want to push as the salesperson. Adding benefit arguments to a single variant (and none to the others) significantly increases the likelihood that the variant thus reinforced will be chosen.

The correct and precise use of customer value represents a very powerful psychological lever in sales and marketing. You can use the customer value strategy to optimize your sales talks, but also your website, newsletters, the texts in your online store, printed documents, and very much more, and make them significantly more effective. Simply put, you will sell more by using the customer value strategy correctly. You can learn how to use it profitably in blog posts linked to the book on the resource page (https://www.romankmenta.com/bap-fragetechniken/).

Objection anticipation

You use objection anticipation by bringing up what the customer is probably thinking but has not (yet) said out loud. You raise the objection before the customer can. This gives you more control over the situation. The customer will feel understood when you "read his mind." He can no longer raise the objection himself - or even doesn't have to - and you can calmly deal with or resolve it using the strategy you have planned.

You can also use this objection anticipation as a question booster in the following form:

- "Can I ask you a **slightly odd (stupid/stupid/outrageous**, etc.) question?"
- "Is it okay if I ask you an **unusual** question?"
- "**You may not want to answer my** next question. May I ask it anyway?"

You build the customer's objection into the question permission as a word or phrase (in bold) and thus warm the customer up to your question. This significantly increases the probability of receiving an honest answer.

Amplify questions body language

You can emphasize questions not only verbally, but also still with body language - through appropriate gestures and facial expressions - in such a way that you produce more or less or even no answers, or also that it evokes certain answers.

Body language reinforcers for closed questions

When you ask closed-ended questions, the possible answers to them - at least strictly speaking - are Yes or No. If you are more likely to want to hear Yes answers (for many closing questions, for example), it helps if you nod very slightly - almost imperceptibly - while asking that question.

To be more likely to hear a no, it's beneficial to shake your head as you would for a no, just not nearly as hard. The customer's subconscious mind understands the message, while his conscious mind is busy with the verbal answer. To encourage the No even more, you can also move one hand palm down at stomach/hip level from the center of your body to diagonally out and down a bit, just as if you were pushing something away.

If you ask the question *"Are there any more questions?" while* giving these body language signals (because you don't have time for more questions, for example), you will get fewer questions than if you do not.

Neither of these body language behaviors should be chosen if you want to get an uninfluenced response, as in the needs assessment of a sales call, for example.

Body language reinforcers for open-ended questions

By definition, open questions are not about yes or no answers, but about getting an answer in the first place that provides as much information as possible. You can encourage this in terms of body language by adopting an open body posture and holding one or both palms open upwards at about stomach level.

Silence as amplifier

One of the most powerful amplifiers of questions ever is neither a word nor a gesture, but simply remaining silent after the question and waiting for the customer to answer. Saying nothing while maintaining expectant eye contact creates very high pressure on your counterpart within seconds. He literally feels compelled to answer.

Attention especially with professional buyers, as you may know, them from industry or trade. They also know the power of silence from seminars in which they are trained. It could degenerate into a duel of silence, which is then lost by the one who has the weaker nerves, or in the concrete case of negotiation, less power.

But now, as announced, to the further question types in alphabetical order.

Requirement questions

Customers have reasons why they choose a product or service. Certain criteria are important to them when making a purchase decision, and some are even particularly important. The offer must (in the case of knock-out criteria) or should fulfill certain requirements. As a salesperson, you should know these.

- *"What is important to you when booking a vacation?"*
- *"What is most important to you when choosing a consultant?"*
- *"What do I need to do to get the job from you?"* (If you want to ask a requirement question in a conclusion-oriented way).
- *"What does our product have to do / what do we have to do to make you choose us?"* (Also asked in a conclusion-oriented manner.)

To get even more information out of this question, it is often advisable to follow up with *"And what else?"* and definitely several times - until you have the impression that the customer has really said everything on this topic.

Observe sequence and emotions

Pay particular attention to the sequence and the intensity or emotionality with which the answers are given. What the customer says first (perhaps very quickly at hand) is very likely to be more important than what comes to mind the third time he asks. The less important criteria are then often packaged in conjunctive, vague formulations or as wishes - e.g. like this:

- *"If the apartment has a second bathroom, that wouldn't be bad."*
- *"I would think it would be even nicer in a vibrant blue."*

If you ask requirement questions openly (like the above examples), the customer may also not have any answers. This is the case if he has never thought about what his buying criteria are. By asking closed or alternative questions, for example, you can help him get started:

- *"Is it important to you that the room has an ocean view?"* (Closed requirement question)
- *"Is good transportation access or as quiet a location as possible more important to you in terms of your new home?"* (alternative question)

Negative requirement questions

Negative requirement questions are a variant of this type of question. These do not ask about the criteria that a product or service should meet, but about those that an offer should not have. Here are a few examples:

- *"What should not happen in the context of the seminar?"*
- *"What would stop you from choosing our offer?"*

By asking questions in this way, customers will often be surprised and have to think first to be able to give you an answer. And that's good. Questions that make customers think are interesting because they often uncover new information.

Motive questions

With the normal requirement questions, you mainly cover the superficial criteria and requirements of your customers - dimensions, colors, duration, etc. Of course, it is very important for you to know these. But it gets really exciting when you go one level deeper and ask about the motives behind them. You do this by asking requirements questions with the following formulation:

- *"You say you prefer option A. May I know why that is?"*
- *"I am curious. Many of our customers choose option B, you prefer option A. I'm interested to know why. Can I ask you?"*
- *"So I can really understand what moves you ... Would you tell me why variant A is so important to you?"*

You already realize that it is appropriate to formulate this inquiry more gently in the form of a *"Why?"* and to work with justifications. Just a simple *"And why?"* would often be too direct and could create inappropriate, unwanted pressure to justify (we have already talked about this earlier with the open questions).

When you dig a little deeper in this way, you often come across the customer's true, fundamental motives for buying. The feature or performance characteristic that the customer named in response to the requirement question is only the outwardly visible manifestation of the motive. An example of this:

In response to the question *"What is important to you when you think about the trip you are planning?"*, your customer said that an all-inclusive offer would be very appealing to him. When asked why, the answer was that he would then no longer have to worry about finding suitable restaurants for lunch and dinner on-site and could thus concentrate entirely on taking advantage of the many activities offered at the hotel. So the customer likes it simple and uncomplicated. The buying motive, "freedom from problems," is behind this.

Another customer may answer the same thing to this requirement question, but the answer to the question of why is: *"You know, I've had bad experiences there several times. First, it is not easy to find halfway good restaurants locally, and if you order à la carte in the hotel, the prices are often outrageously high. An all-inclusive deal is usually much cheaper."* The criterion is the same, but the motive behind it, the customer's actual need, is quite different - in this case, "saving money."

Knowing these needs and addressing them precisely in the form of benefit arguments is enormously important in sales (as well as in marketing) and a highly effective lever for higher sales figures.

You can read about what the needs are and how to address them in blog posts found in the resources section (https://www.romankmenta.com/bap-fragetechniken/) for the book.

Questioning needs

In response to requirement questions à la *"What is important to you if you ...?"* or even when asking why in order to get to the bottom of true needs, customers often also answer with nominalizations (adjectives made into nouns, i.e. nouns) or their answers are not so clear that you would understand what exactly they mean:

- *"Safety is important to me"*
- *"Above all, I have to keep control of the process."*
- *"Variety is an important theme for us on vacation."*

Answers to the *"What is important to you when you ...?"* question often go something like this. I could also describe these terms, such as security, control, variety, etc., as customer values. However, values on their own may not have significant meaning. The true meaning of these values lies in the so-called fulfillment conditions. Security, for example, may be important to you and me. Nevertheless, you probably understand something quite different by it than I do. Financial security, physical security, job security, reliability about something specific? Security can mean a lot of things. It's the same with your customers. Therefore, don't stop asking here just yet and be fobbed off with this term. You need to question these fulfillment conditions for nominalization.

You can do this, for example, in the following form:

- *"May I ask what you mean by safety?"* (With a short question permission before)

- *"To help me understand even better what you need, may I ask what you mean by safety*?" (With a justification and permission to ask)
- *"What does safety mean to you?*
- *"When you say safety, what exactly do you mean by that?"* (As a concretization question)
- *"How do you feel when you have security?"* (Emotion-related question)
- *"What exactly would need to be met for safety to be a reality for you?"* (As a concretization question)

The answers that come to such questions are then much more concrete and at the same time, much more informative and helpful for you.

Confirmation questions/checking questions/inspection questions

Confirmation questions (often called checking questions or control questions) serve several different functions in a sales conversation. Depending on the situation and the goal, they serve to,

- to secure or clarify information,
- Collect jas or also
- Obtain views of the customer and
- Bring more interaction into conversations

Often perform several of these functions simultaneously.

Secure information

Whenever you are not sure whether you have understood something correctly, you can or must work with control questions.

- *"Is that a good fit for you?"*
- *"Did I understand that correctly?"*
- *"Is that what you wanted?"*

Collect Jas

Ultimately, in sales, the goal is to get the customer to say yes - to a proposal, a solution, or an offer. To achieve this, it's helpful to collect lots of little "yeses" throughout the conversation to warm them up for the final "yes." Control questions are an effective way to achieve this. The point, in this case, is not to learn something new or to clear up an ambiguity but to get the customer to say yes again and again. It must, therefore, always be a closed question. Therefore, only ask this type of control question if you know that the customer will answer it in the affirmative (because they have already expressed exactly this desire or requirement in response to a requirements question, for example).

The checking questions you can ask in the process are often the same as those you can ask when securing information:

- *"Is that okay with you?"*
- *"Does this meet your needs?"*
- *"And that was your wish, if I remember correctly." (Strictly a statement)*

Obtain the customer's views

If your goal with the control question is not only to clarify a specific point or collect yeses, but (in addition) to get the customer's perspective on a particular proposal or feature and thus obtain more information, then you should ask the confirmation question openly:

- *"What do you say?"*
- *"What do you think?"*
- *"What do you think of that?"*

Bring more interaction into conversations

Particularly in phases in which there is a risk that the salesperson will speak too much and the customer too little - such as during the presentation of products or services - confirmation questions are very suitable for bringing more interaction into the conversation. After all, the customer should also have his say in these phases.

Open-ended questions are also recommended for this purpose, as they increase the likelihood of a lengthy response from the customer. In this way, you can repeatedly ask checking questions - after naming product features, suggestions, etc. (ideally supported by benefit arguments).

- *"This bathtub is overlong with 2.10 meters inside dimension. This has the advantage that even you, as a very tall person, can stretch out in it and thus enjoy the warm water all over your body. What do you think?"*

For example, checking questions can be used in a product presentation. Basically, every question that is asked automatically brings additional interaction into the conversation and increases the customer's share of the conversation.

Emotion-related questions

Do emotions and business go together? Sometimes you could get the impression that emotions have no place in business. Exactly the opposite is true. Especially in sales, emotions are a very important factor for success. Some people think that good parts of purchasing decisions are made on the basis of emotions. In my view, this is not true. Rather, I maintain that all buying decisions are ultimately made emotionally. However, we often try to wrap our emotional decisions in a factual, rational cloak in order to make them appear more reasonable to others.

So instead of trying to push emotions out of sales (which wouldn't work anyway) and remaining completely factual, it is much better to consciously use emotions as a lever for success.

One variation in doing this is to ask emotion-related questions, such as *"How do you feel about this solution?"* But what exactly are these used for in sales? Why and when can or should you ask them? In what might be a very matter-of-fact and sober sales conversation, emotions that you bring into the conversation in the form of questions have the following benefits:

- You learn new things from the customer or even completely new sides and facets to known things.
    - *"Quite apart from the factual arguments, how do you feel about the idea of implementing it in this way?"*
    - *"What do you really hate about the current situation? What gets on your nerves?"* (Asking about negative emotions can also be very enriching and revealing).
    - *"How do you think your employees will feel about working with this solution in the future?"* (Emotion-based, circular question - more on this later).
- You may get to know the real motives (better).
    - *"If you feel inside yourself: What are you really about?"*
- Through the answers the customer gives you to your emotion-related questions, they themselves likewise gain more clarity about what they want and why they want it.
    - *"Is it more the anger about the current solutions that drives you, or the joy of a new solution that allows you to be much more relaxed about the future?"* (Alternative, emotion-based question)
- A conversation that might be stuck on the factual level gets moving again. This could also be a price negotiation, for example, in which the salesperson

and the customer cannot reach an agreement. To put this in a picture: You are driving on a highway, and the factual lane is blocked by a traffic jam. By switching to the emotional lane, you have enough space to move forward again.

- *"Price as a number is only one side of the coin. The other is the question: How do you feel about the idea of saying yes to my offer?"*
- *"Maybe it's not the amount that bothers you at all, but the feeling of not having achieved your goal and thus having failed. Is that so?"* (Closed, emotion-related question)
- *"Something is obviously bothering you about this? What does your gut say? What is it?"*

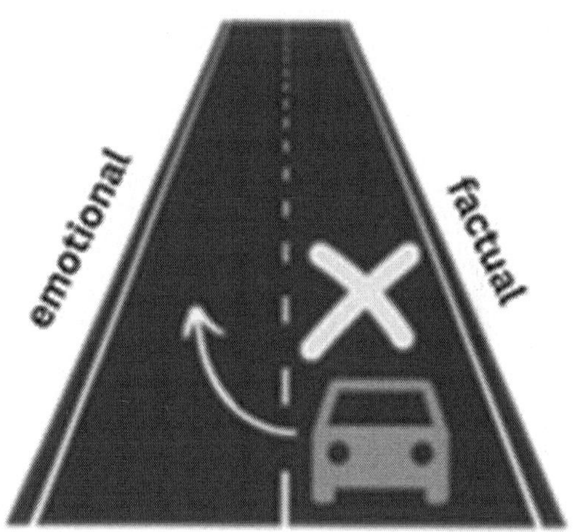

In coaching - that's where I borrowed for this type of question - we work very much and successfully with emotion-related questions.

Fact questions/information questions

In some phases of a sales talk - especially in the needs assessment - pure fact questions or information questions can be used very well. These are important, although relatively unspectacular. They ask for numbers, data and facts of all kinds that relate to the customer's wishes and needs with regard to your products or service. These can be asked openly, closed, or alternatively.

Some examples of this:

- *"How long do you plan to be gone?"*
- *"Where exactly is the pain in your back?"*
- *"Do you need the printout in black and white or color?"*
- *"How much storage do you need?"*
- *"Who usually rides in the car?"*
- *"Do you need a trailer hitch?"*
- *"What is the budget you have allocated for this project?"*
- *"Are you paying cash?"*

The possibilities for asking fact questions are almost endless. They are probably among the most frequently asked questions in sales conversations - presumably because they have to be asked in order to be able to create an offer at all.

Counter questions

Counter-questions are much more interesting from a sales psychology and conversation point of view. How do they work? Your customer asks a question, and you either ask a counter-question immediately and without answering, or you attach a counter-question to the answer.

Counter question without answer

- Customer: *"Does the pizza come with spinach?"*
  Salesman: *"Do you want them with spinach?"*
  (A counter question as a closing question)

Counter question with answer

- Customer: *"What control options does this device offer?"*
  Salesman: *"There is manual control, semi-automatic control, or fully automatic control, where the computer takes over all the work steps. Which do you prefer?"*

Counter-questions do not have a good reputation (especially if they are used extremely and too frequently), but they fulfill extremely important functions in the context of leading a conversation. As mentioned earlier, the saying goes, *"He who asks, leads!"* And who should - at least by and large - "lead" a sales conversation? That's right, the salesperson. So if the customer asks questions (which of course, he is allowed to do and should do because it shows that he is interested) and the salesperson answers them exclusively, the customer has taken the lead.

In order to regain control of the conversation, the counter-question (as demonstrated in the example) is the method of choice. You can use the variant without an answer (if the situation allows and you do not do this too often) or the somewhat gentler variant with an answer before the question.

Hypothetical questions

Even more exciting in terms of sales psychology, because they can be used in an extremely wide variety of ways, are hypothetical questions à la *"What if ...?"*. Sales conversations can, as mentioned, get stuck at times. You have maneuvered yourself as a salesperson or customer into a dead end and cannot move forward and sometimes not back. Or you or the customer are facing a hurdle that seems impossible to overcome. Such hurdles can be overcome with hypothetical questions - mentally, in the first step. This often leads to a solution that is not purely mental, but can also work in the real world. An example of this:

- Customer: *"I think the concept is very good, but it clearly exceeds our budget. We can't implement it."*
  Salesperson: *"Assuming budget was not an issue, would you implement the concept as proposed?"*
  Customer: *"Yes, I would."*
  Seller: *"What would be the advantages for you?"*
  Customer: *"We could speed up the processes in our production."*
  Seller: *"And who would benefit from that?"*
  Customer: *"The whole company, I would think."*
  Salesperson: *"How much money would that save you?"*

> Customer: *"I think a good 1,000 euros per day. I can see what they're getting at ... But the budget is still not there."*
> Salesperson: *"Let me ask you one more question ... If it had been possible to get the budget for it, what would have happened so that the budget would be available?"* (Admittedly a somewhat complex question, which certainly requires the customer to think for a moment).
> Customer: *"Our general manager would have had a good day and approved the budget."*
> Salesperson: *"If there was one thing that would give your CEO a good day, what would it be?"* ...

Whether the budget will be provided and the vendor will get the job, I don't know either. Let's just assume a happy ending. What the example shows is how you can use hypothetical questions to continue the conversation even in situations with a seemingly insurmountable obstacle and - possibly - come up with completely new ideas and solutions. The *"What if ...?"* question can be used in very many scenarios and is very helpful.

A few formulations for it:

- *"If you could decide on your own, would you buy it?"* (Hypothetical closing question)
- *"If you had complete freedom of choice, what would you want for your new home?"*
- *"Suppose you were to receive a five percent return from this investment every year; what would you do*

with it?" (By this, the salesperson suggests that the investment offered will yield five percent).

Questions of this type can be best used to put your customer in a desirable state or an emotionally positive mood associated with a target state. You are sending the customer on a little journey to a time when they have already bought your product or service and are enjoying it:

- *"I know that seems hard to fund right now, but if you imagine - just for a moment - that it could. How would that feel?"* (Emotion-based hypothetical question)
- *"If you imagined you already owned this great vehicle and took it out for its first ride, who would you take with you?"*
- *"Often when deciding on an apartment, it helps to imagine what it would be like to already live there. Let's say you were having a party in your new apartment. Who would all be there and what would the visitors say about the new apartment?"*

Hypothetical questions can yield results even if they sound a bit strange:

- Salesperson: *"What is important to you when making a purchase decision like this?"*
  Customer: *"I don't know. I haven't really thought about that yet."*
  Seller: *"I see. Suppose you knew. What would it be?"*
  Customer: *"Well, X wouldn't be bad and if there was also Y ..."*

Used in this way, hypothetical questions can stimulate the flow of the customer's thoughts.

Concretization questions

Humans tend to use generalizations (generalizations) frequently in our language. So often that we no longer even notice them:

- always, never, rarely
- the customers, the Germans
- the starters, the electric cars

Our language is peppered with generalizations. Who are "the Germans"? Are they all really the same? What does "always" mean? Is there never an exception? Whenever you as a salesperson hear generalizations, you should become very alert, because it is often important to get more specific. Apart from generalizations, statements from customers are also very vague and unspecific at many points in the sales conversation.

- In the needs assessment, *"The suitcase should just be big enough."*
- On price talk, *"It's too expensive for me."*
- As an objection, *"But that's been a long time."*
- In closing, *"I'll think about it."*
- In closing, *"We still need to discuss this internally."*

Customers often express themselves in vague or ambiguous ways, leaving you as a salesperson unsure of how to proceed.

In order to gain more clarity and move forward with the sale, concretization questions can be enormously helpful.

You could formulate these to fit the examples above like this:

- In the needs assessment, *"The suitcase should just be big enough."*
    - Seller: *"How big is big enough?"*
- In the price conversation, *"That's too expensive for me?"*
    - Seller: *"What exactly do you mean by too expensive?"*
- As an objection, *"But that's been a long time."*
    - Seller: *"What is the maximum time?*
- In closing, *"I'll think about it."*
    - Salesperson: *"What exactly do you have to think about?"*
- In closing, *"We still need to discuss this internally."*
    - Salesperson: *"Who exactly is all involved in this decision?"*

Not always, but often formulations such as.

- "What exactly ...?"
- "How much exactly ...?"
- "When exactly ...?"

These and other combinations of question words with "exactly" can be used very well to get the customer to be more specific in his statement.

In more difficult cases where your customer doesn't have a concrete answer or doesn't want to tell you (in a price discussion, for example), you can help the customer by providing areas to be more specific.

An example of this from a price discussion:

- Customer: *"It's too expensive."*
  Seller: *"What exactly do you mean by too expensive?"*
  Customer: *"I can't tell you that. But it's well above our budget."*
  Salesperson: *"Exactly how much would I have to accommodate you?"*
  Customer: *"I suggest you see what you can do."*
  Salesperson: *"I'm happy to do that, but to know if that's even possible, I would need to know a dimension. Are we talking about three, four or five percent?"*
  Customer: *"Well, it should be five percent."*

A conversation sequence could run like this or something similar, in which you, as the salesperson, elicit the customer's price ideas with concretization questions and ranges that you specify - if that's what you want (this doesn't always have to be the best strategy).

Reduce emotions

A very important area of application for concretization questions is when the customer is too emotional, or the conversation is very emotional, and you want to bring more objectivity into the conversation. They are, so to speak, the antithesis of emotion-related questions. With concretization questions, you switch from the congested emotional lane to the free objective lane on the highway that your conversation represents (you remember the image we used for this in the emotion-related questions).

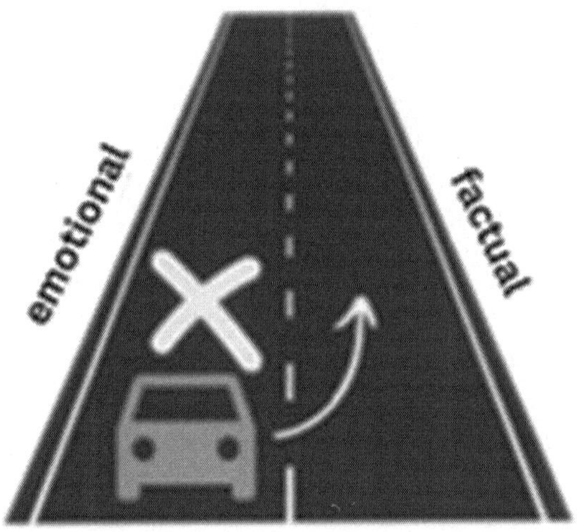

This is often very helpful in the course of complaints, because customers often react highly emotionally - a state that is not very conducive to a solution. You have to take emotions out of it in order to de-escalate. So ask - after a phase in which you have understood the customer and his problem in great detail and empathically:

- *"What exactly happened?"*

- *"How exactly does the problem manifest itself?"*
- *"When exactly does the error occur?"*
- *"What exactly bothers you about it?"*

Used with flair in the right place, you can literally flip the switch with concretization questions and transport the customer into a different emotional state.

Solution questions

Solution questions are a variant of hypothetical questions that come into play when you want to make a solution palatable to your customer before you offer it to him directly. They are always very suitable to use when you have encountered a problem in a previous conversation with the customer for which you have a solution.

For example, you can formulate solution questions as follows:

- *"How would you benefit if the turnaround time in production was 20 minutes instead of 25?"*
- *"Assuming there was a solution to this bottleneck, what exactly would that change for you?"*
- *"How much additional revenue could you generate if you found a way to get three additional leads every day?"*
- *"If there was an apartment with a balcony for the same price as this one, how interesting would that be?"*

In doing so, you should make sure that the question is not posed too "flatly". This can be the case if the solution that is held out in prospect is so attractive that any halfway sensible customer naturally has to want it. Then a (hidden) catch is very quickly suspected in the whole thing.

- *"If I could promise to double your return on investment without increasing your risk ... How would that be for you?"*

... would be a solution question that could seem very "borderline" for the customer.

Normally, the customer's answer will be a positive, pleasant one, since you are holding out the prospect of a solution to his problem. By their very nature, solution questions are usually found from the middle to the final phase of a sales conversation.

Meta questions

Meta questions are a type of question that also comes more from the corner of coaching, but can also be used very well in sales. Imagine you are talking to a customer and notice that the conversation is not going well. He avoids you, doesn't really listen, seems to be disinterested, behaves dismissively or else brings a striking number of objections and is almost aggressive. In such situations, it is often pointless to simply continue with the conversation. You know that it will lead nowhere.

It is wise to take a moment to pause the conversation and mentally step back to gain a clear understanding of the situation, whether it is going well or not. The cause of a conversation not going well could be related to the relationship between you and the customer or it could be that the customer has other issues or problems that are hindering their focus.

This is precisely what you need to determine, as without it, you are aware that your conversation will not reach a productive end and you will not achieve your goal. This is where the so-called meta questions come in - they don't relate to the content of the sales conversation, but rather to the conversation itself.

A few examples of meta questions:

- *"Sorry to interrupt for a moment, but I get the feeling that your mind is not on the game. Is that so?"* (Closed meta question)
- *"It seems to me that something is disturbing you quite massively and fundamentally. What is it?"* (Open meta question)
- *"Is it our offer or have I done something completely wrong that makes you seem so disinterested?"* (Alternative meta question)

Your customer now has the following options to answer this question:

- He admits that you are right with your assumption and tells you what bothers him (if necessary, also about your behavior) or concerns him. This gives you very important information that you would not have received if you had stayed in the conversation instead of dropping out and questioning the relationship or the conversation. On this basis, you now have the opportunity to clarify the issues and objections that have been expressed (if they are with you) and then continue with the conversation much better than before.

- The second possibility is that your interlocutor does not share your concerns or even understands what you mean and how you come to such an assumption. This may be the truth. But it may also be that your customer does not want to tell you the real reasons for his behavior in the conversation. Often, however, he will still "pull himself together" in the further course of the conversation, so that even in this case the conversation can continue more easily. Of course, it is much better if the customer discloses his reasons to you - as in variant 1.

What it takes to use this type of question is, above all, courage. Bringing up hidden topics, especially if they could be on the relationship level, does not correspond to our normal behavior - neither professionally nor privately. But what will happen to your conversation if you don't? It will ripple along on the surface. You will somehow bring it to a close - even if only out of politeness - but it will not produce the results you want. So what do you have to lose?

If there are unspoken objections on the part of the customer, especially if they are important ones, it is almost always better to bring them to light. Because only if you know them, you can solve them.

Follow-up question n

If a lot has already been said, but you are not sure whether there might not be something exciting to learn from the customer on a particular topic, you can ask a demand. These are basically quite simple in their form:

- *"What else is there that's important to you that we haven't talked about?"*
- *"What else can you think of?"*

By asking this open, suggestive form of the question, you are implying that there is something more. It will more often elicit further responses than the closed variant:

- *"Is there anything else you can think of to say about that?"*

Again, the customer might think of something else, but the likelihood is less than with open-ended questioning. So if you really want to get further answers, then ask open-ended questions. If you only want to ask a follow-up question for the sake of form, but do not expect or want any further answers, then ask a closed question.

As mentioned earlier in the book (for the open and closed questions), you can also reinforce these questions using body language in one direction or the other (head and hand movements).

And if that's still not enough for you, you can also ask one or more follow-up questions to the follow-up question:

- *"And what else?"*

- *"And what else can you think of beyond that?"*

Ask them as long or as often (with slightly changing wording) until you think that really everything has been said that needs to be said at the moment. And stop before you run the risk of annoying the customer - a risk that is not great, however, as I know from my own sales practice.

Ecology Issues

Ecology issues have - as the name suggests - something to do with the environment. However, they are not primarily about nature, but about the human environment. In this way, you ask how a proposal that the customer accepts or a solution, product or service that he or she buys affects his or her environment - especially, but not only, the people around him or her.

Everything has advantages and disadvantages in life and in business. There is a price to pay for everything, often not in the form of money. For you as a salesperson, it can be very important in some situations to check together with the customer whether the advantages that the customer has with your service or product outweigh the disadvantages. If you do not do this, it can lead to cancellations, complaints, and problems of all kinds, or the sale may not be concluded at all.

In the simplest form, you can ask quite openly:

- *"If you implement it this way, what will be the advantages and disadvantages?"*
- *"What is the impact and on whom if you achieve your goal with it?"*

- *"How would people around you react if you chose our solution."*

In this way, you ask, if you are seriously interested in the advantages and disadvantages. *"Does it make sense to bring up the possible disadvantages to the customer? Isn't that counterproductive? After all, it could kill the deal."* you might rightly ask. Yes, it makes sense in that by asking such questions, you bring to light the potential downsides that lurk in the background as a threat to your deal. These dangers are nothing more than objections that you can deal with - but only if you know them. You can find solutions to them. It is much better for the closing of the deal to know the objections and discuss them with the customer than for the customer to think about them without you.

But it's not so much about the objections on the product itself (the underperformance, the color that doesn't fit perfectly, the delivery time that's too long), but the objections that other people around him might raise, or the adverse effects of a product on his physical environment when he uses it.

For example, suppose the customer who wants to buy a motorcycle replies that it could be that his wife is accusing him of spending too much money on such toys as a motorcycle. In that case, the salesperson could suggest a leasing option. This won't make the motorcycle any cheaper overall, but the monthly installments will make it seem much cheaper, possibly taking the wind out of his wife's sails of criticism.

You can intensify this search for objections and possible problems with the customer even more by asking very specifically about disadvantages and, in doing so, also deliberately making the customer think of certain people or circumstances. This is especially important if these people are not present or are not directly involved in the buying process.

- *"Everything in life has its drawbacks. What could your family possibly find wrong with this solution?"*
    - *"And what else?"* (Follow-up questions can also be combined with ecology questions).
- *"How will your neighbors react if you suddenly have a pool?"*
- *"Will your friends be pleased when you tell them you have chosen this solution?"* (Also possible as a closed question)
- *"Will your parents approve or disapprove of your decision?"* (An alternative ecology question)
    - *"And what exactly will you object to?"* (Connected with a follow-up question)

It is not just a matter of finding solutions to the potential objections - sometimes, these do not even exist. It is often sufficient or even much more beneficial to prepare the customer mentally for the objections, to strengthen his back and to provide him with arguments or behavioral patterns on how he will deal with the concerns or criticism of others about his purchase decision. This removes a huge, usually unspoken obstacle to buying. If a customer has concerns or even fears about the reaction of their partner, friends, neighbors, or parents, that's often the reason something isn't purchased.

These concerns can sometimes be a bit embarrassing for customers, so they will only tell you about them if you ask them specifically (assuming a certain level of trust).

To stay with the motorcycle example, which our client's wife might have reservations about:

- Salesman: *"What do you think your wife will say when you treat yourself to this motorcycle?"*
  Customer: *"Well, if you ask me about it, she won't be pleased."*
  Salesperson: "And why is that?"
  Customer: *"She's afraid I might get hurt. Especially since our neighbor was in the hospital for three months last year after a motorcycle accident."*
  Seller: *"Mmmh. I can understand and sympathize with that. How will you react when your wife complains that you bought the bike?"*
  Customer: *"I will explain to her that I ride carefully."*
  Seller: *"Will this do?"*
  Customer (grinning): *"Probably not."*
  Salesperson: *"What else could we do to take the wind out of her sails a little?"*
  Customer: *"Our neighbor had a helmet on, but no protective clothing at all."*
  Salesman: *"That is to say, if you are well equipped, your wife will be reassured?"*
  Customer: *"A little bit, at least."*
  Salesperson: *"Well, then I would suggest that we take a look right now at what you need to make your wife less afraid for you."*

In this way, such hidden objections from others can be used as an argument for additional sales, for example. Incidentally, an interesting additional sale for such cases would be accident insurance and life insurance, at least to take the wind out of the customer's wife's sails with regard to the financial arguments in the event of an accident.

This salesman could even go one step further - a very big one, admittedly - by trying to win the woman as a customer, too. With what argument? I always had a queasy feeling, sometimes sheer fear, when I rode along on friends' motorcycles in my youth. When I rode myself, on the other hand, I felt safe. Admittedly, the idea of turning the customer's wife from an opponent into a customer is quite far-fetched in this case, but it would be worth a try.

After the add-on sale with our motorcycle customer is complete, the salesperson might return to the subject of his wife's fear once again, not only to reinforce the customer's back, but to "inoculate" him and thus immunize him against his wife's criticism.

- Seller: *"And will your wife be satisfied now and give her OK to your purchase?"*
  Customer: *"Well, more satisfied."*
  Seller: *"And what if you still has something against your great bike? Will you then stand here with me again tomorrow to give it all back to me?"*
  Customer: *"No, I won't."*
  Salesman: *"Sure?"*
  Customer: "*Yes, for sure. After all, I can still buy what I want with my money."*

> Salesman (smiling): *"Well, that's good then. After all, I don't want to be the cause of relationship problems."*

Mentally prepared in this way, the customer will meet his wife's objections much more easily and the likelihood of a cancellation (if legally possible at all) is now almost zero. The customer has assured the seller several times that he will not let his wife talk him out of the motorcycle.

If you want to take a tougher stance on ecology issues, you can ask the question in such a way that it is no longer a question, but an assertion in question form:

- *"And your wife? She probably won't be thrilled that you're buying a motorcycle, will she?*

... an admittedly very direct and somewhat harsh question or announcement. You could make it a little softer by asking it more indirectly and pushing others forward as reasons for the question:

- *"Even though I've been riding motorcycles for so long now, my wife still gets scared when I go out. How is yours, if I may ask so indiscreetly?"*
- *"Statistics show that many men don't buy after all because their partners object to motorcycles. How high is this risk in your case?"*

One of my clients, a seller of prefabricated homes, took the idea even further to reduce or avoid cancellations, which can certainly be a problem in the industry. When a customer, who seemed a bit unsure, wanted to buy and had signed the sales contract, he would say the following:

- Seller: *"I'm very happy that you decided to buy this great house, but honestly, I still have my doubts."*
  Customer (astonished): *"What doubts?"*
  Seller: *"I'm not sure you won't change your mind and call me tomorrow and cancel the purchase."*
  Customer: *"No, certainly not."*
  Salesman (smiling): *"Then let's make a bet. I'll bet you a bottle of good champagne that you'll back out of the purchase. If you don't, you'll not only get your great new house, but you'll also get my wager from me - a bottle of champagne."*

The customer, of course, had no risk in the bet. The seller would have given him the bottle anyway, as a gift for completing the purchase. But this way, he could reduce the risk of cancellation with a wink.

As you can see, ecology questions are much more fruitful than they may first appear, and include a wealth of applications in your sales pitches.

Paradoxical questions

Paradoxical questions are rarely if ever, found in sales. At first glance, they seem too exotic to many - perhaps even to you - to be able to use them in sales. Precisely for this reason, they are an exciting instrument that should not be missing from your toolbox in sales.

What am I even talking about? Instead of asking about what the customer expects, ask about what they don't expect. Think of the exact opposite of what the customer probably wants and wrap that up in a question:

- *"What can you do to derail the project?"*
- *"What do you need to do to get your wife to file for divorce tomorrow?"* (a couples therapist might ask.)
- *"What do you need to do to sleep worse?"* (a doctor might ask.)
- *"Photographers have probably taken a lot of bad photos of you in the past, too. What do I have to do to take even worse ones?"* (a photographer might ask before the shoot).
- *"What would you have to change about your business that would make no one even want to work here?"*

As strange as these questions may sound, they have a lot of potentials to bring new insights. Often, the same factors that make something worse or cause it to fail are the same ones that can be used to make it better and lead to success. Often - but not always - it is simply the exact opposite of what needs to be done. Interestingly, people - including customers - often know what they don't want or should do, but not what they want or should do. By asking paradoxical questions, you can reach your goal via a - very productive - detour.

Problem questions and problem deepening questions

In recent years, almost a phobia has developed about using the word "problem" in communication, especially in sales. Instead, people speak of "challenges," "hurdles," or even "tasks." Reframing is the method of replacing one word with another that has a slightly different meaning, and it can also be used in questioning as you will read shortly. While reframing can be useful in communication by replacing a negative word with a more positive one, this should not lead to the assumption that problems in sales are inherently bad and must be hidden.

On the contrary: problems, or more precisely the customer's problems, are even very good and a real sales turbo if - and this is the essential prerequisite - you have the solution for them. If they are urgent and big problems, that's all the better. To use an image for this: If your customer is dying of thirst and you are the only one far and wide who can sell him water, then you can close very quickly and sell at almost any price.

Now it is true that the problems of your customers do not always have to be so large and pressing. Only very few customers are "dying of thirst". Often they are just small problems, little problems, so to speak. Still, it pays to go looking for them and know what they are. And that's what you do with problem questions.

These are basically quite simple:

- *"What problems do you have in this area?"* (If you want to ask very directly).
- *"What didn't go ideally with your previous solution?"* (If you want to approach the topic a little more gently).
- *"What torments you and keeps you from sleeping when you wake up at three in the morning thinking about your business?"* (If you want to make the customer perhaps smile and in any case think).
- *"What topics do you discuss intensively when it comes to your logistics?"*

- *"What challenges are you currently facing in recruiting?"*
- *"What would - if you get this solved - take you a big step forward?"* (Also a question that is likely to make the customer think a little longer).
- *"What's stopping you from launching a new product line?"*

Of course, problem questions should be asked with tact (especially if you formulate them very directly) and need a solid relationship basis and a fair amount of trust. *"What are the issues you are arguing about with your partner?"* is a question you are unlikely to answer to a stranger on the street, but would virtually expect from your couples therapist or coach.

Now that we have discussed some question types, I would like to take the example of problem questions to discuss the combination of different question types. As mentioned at the beginning, an excellently implemented question technique combines and interweaves a wide variety of question types in a meaningful way. This creates variety for the customer and gives you significantly more insight.

Question combination with problem questions

- **Problem questions and follow-up questions**
  Following up problem questions with follow-up questions such as *"And what else?"* makes a lot of sense in many cases and unearths more problems or

more information about a problem already mentioned.

- **Problem questions and concretization questions** *"What exactly do you mean when you say that the performance of your sales force sometimes reaches its limits?"* These and similar concretization questions help to create even more clarity for you (but also for the customer).

- **Problem questions and ecology questions** *"How does this problem affect your family?"* is a question that can not only create insight, but make the client even more aware of the severity of the problem or its urgency.

- **Problem questions and emotion-related questions** *"How does this make you feel when you think about these problems you've had with it over and over in the past?"* This emotion-related question is also likely to increase the customer's awareness of the problem because more emotions come into play.

- **Problem questions and hypothetical questions** *"Although you said earlier that you had no problems with it, I would still like to ask you, if you had problems, what would they probably be?"* This type of question is suitable for letting the customer find problems after all, with a hypothetical question, which he may not have thought of at all or to get him talking if he is rather reticent.

- **Problem questions and fact questions**
  "How often do you wake up during the night? And when?" are fact questions/information questions that a doctor could ask his customer in a sales talk (yes, doctors also sell or should see their patients as customers).

These are just a few examples from the question types discussed so far, to show you how well all these questions can be combined with each other and to give you a taste for doing the same in your sales conversations. Thus warmed up, it will be easy for you to make such combinations with the following question types as well.

Problem deepening questions

But problem questions are only or only the first step when it comes to exploring the customer's problems. As mentioned, better than simple problems are big and pressing problems. With so-called problem-deepening questions, you can make the customer's problems bigger and thus more pressing and meaningful to him. They also help, in combination with the normal problem questions, to create a solid awareness of the problem in the customer in the first place, when he may not have been aware of his problems at all.

- *"What impact does this problem have on your business?"*
- *"How much do these delays you're struggling with cost you every day?"* (You can also add up the costs over weeks, months, and years to make the perceived problem seem much bigger).

- *"What have you already paid so far for not being able to clear this hurdle yet?"*

Problem deepening questions - figuratively speaking - drill a little into the wound that you have uncovered with the problem questions. This can be painful (for the customer) and is therefore only recommended (and morally justifiable) if you also have the solution to the problem. But big and painful problems are - as hard as it may sound - the basis for many a corporate empire and even entire industries.

And yes, great wishes that providers fulfill are also a good basis for business. But sometimes desires and problems are exactly the same thing - just viewed from two sides. When push comes to shove - I maintain - pressing problems are even better salespeople. However, this should by no means stop you from getting to the bottom of your customers' wishes as well - with open requirement questions, hypothetical questions, and so on. You already have plenty of suitable tools for this in this book.

Problem questions and solution questions

As you may have guessed yourself, problem questions and the solution questions discussed earlier in the question alphabet have a strong relationship of proximity. Just as a solution belongs to a problem, the solution questions belong to the problem questions. After you have worked out the customer's problem by means of problem questions and have created a strong awareness of the problem in the customer, you can now present your solution to him.

This presentation can either be direct or introduced by means of solution questions:

- *"If there was a solution to the issue we discussed, how interesting would that be to you?"* (Open solution question)
- *"What should a solution to this problem cost to make it interesting to you?"* (A special form of the solution question, in which you assume that there is a solution).
- *"Can I assume that you can handle this problem and are open to a solution?"* (Closed solution question)

In these examples, the solution question has nothing to do with the content of the solution itself. It warms up the customer for the solution, makes him curious and - depending on the situation - also hopeful by holding out the prospect of an end to his problems. What's more, you pick up another yes.

You will get another yes if you continue as follows:

- *"Well, then, I have a proposal that will be very interesting to you. May I show it to you?"*

It is a purely rhetorical question (which I will also discuss in detail), but the customer is very likely to answer yes at this point. Therefore, use solution questions to follow up on problem questions and prepare your customer for the presentation of the solution.

Reframing questions /reinterpretation-questions

I have already briefly mentioned the term "reframing". However, reframing is such an important and powerful communication technique that it deserves much more attention. And it is represented in this book because it also has a lot to do with questions.

Reframing can also be translated as "reinterpretation". It's about giving terms - usually those with negative connotations - a more positive or even positive meaning. You can do this in two ways, by means of

- Context reframing or
- Meaning reframing.

Context reframing

In context reframing, you put something in a different context, setting, or environment to change the meaning for the positive.

- A very overweight man (overweight has a negative association in our country) has the best chance to become a successful sumo wrestler in Japan.
- A dry and hot summer is bad for plants, but the nice weather has advantages for tourism.

You could say "context reframing" is looking for benefits and positive effects that something has in other situations and circumstances. *"What is this an opportunity for?"* is the question you can ask yourself or the customer when looking for an appropriate context reframing. In what situations do the disadvantages of your product or service have advantages for the customer.

You could do this in the form of a statement - *"But in return you have an advantage if you ..."* - or even formulate it as a question:

- *"What advantages does the extra length of our parts give you in assembly?"* (Even if the long parts are a bit more difficult to produce, they save time in assembly - a new context).
- *"What's in it for you if you have to wait longer than scheduled for your delivery?"*
- *"At what stage of the sale is it good for this salesperson to be impatient?"* (The other context could be, for example, making an appointment or even closing).

Although the result of the question - the customer's answer - may be the same in terms of content that you would have packaged into a statement, it is quite different. In case of formulating it as a question, you give the customer the opportunity to come up with the advantages of your product or solution in other situations by himself.

Anything you can say, you can ask.

And asking is usually better than telling. The answers that the customer gives himself are always better than those of the salesperson, who, of course, MUST say good things about his offer. But that doesn't mean you can't use context reframing wrapped in statements. In some situations, such as when the customer can't know the answer, this can make a lot of sense and be the quickest approach.

As you have probably already noticed, the examples discussed are mostly about objections that the customer brings. And yes, questions in general - and reframing questions in particular - are an excellent way to deal with objections.

So, phrased very generally as a standard question that you can use in all sorts of sales situations and proposals, a context reframing might be:

- *"Where does X (the customer's disadvantage/objection) give you an advantage/benefit?"*

We will discuss the topic of questions in objection handling in more detail in the second part of the book.

Meaning reframing

Even simpler and more universally applicable is meaning reframing.

Nothing has meaning outside of that which we give it.

The meaning of everything only arises from the fact that we ascribe such a meaning to it. We find cheese delicious and the Chinese disgusting. For some people, having nothing to do has a positive connotation because they associate it with relaxation and recreation; for others, it means boredom. In meaning reframing, you give terms and words a different meaning by using different terms and words - ones that customers associate positively, rather than ones they use that have negative connotations.

For example, I've gotten into the habit of asking people who complain about stress and being busy (negative connotation), *"That means you're not bored?"* which is a more positive connotation. You might just as well ask, *"That means business is good?" if* you are reasonably sure that it is, so as not to put your foot in your mouth (busy even though business is not good).

The simplest form of meaning reframing is to replace individual words with more positive ones.

- expensive >> valuable/high-priced
- difficult >> not quite easy / challenging
- bad/stupid etc. >> interesting (fits for many things)
- Problem / Difficulty >> Task / Challenge / Hurdle
- Stress >> much to do
- pissed off >> (very) upset
- haphazard >> flexible
- rigid >> strong/resistant/rooted
- disgusting >> exotic
- unsuspecting >> unbiased
- sour >> natural

With reframing, you must, of course, proceed with a lot of tact. The distance in meaning must not be too great and should be adapted to the situation. What does that mean? If the customer perceives something as a really big problem and you reframe it as an opportunity too early in the conversation, it can backfire. The step from a really big problem to a hurdle to overcome is a much smaller one, but still one in the right direction. And at some point, after a few more steps in the conversation, the customer may even be ready to see his big problem as an opportunity, but that often takes time. Sometimes much more time than is available in a single conversation.

So how do you package meaning reframings into questions? The easiest way to do this is with feedback/comprehension questions (we will take a closer look at these):

- Customer: *"This is really a problem for me."*
  Salesperson: *"So, if I understand you correctly, you are facing a situation that is not easy to solve?"*

- Customer: *"But this is expensive what you offer here?"*
  Seller: *"Did you want something CHEAP?"* (This is also a meaning refaiming. Expensive is in relation to something CHEAP - pronounced with a hint of contempt in the voice - the more positive word).

Although this book primarily focuses on questioning techniques, it's important to note that the knowledge you have gained about reframing can be applied to statements as well. It's not always necessary to use a question to reframe a situation.

- Customer: *"I find this delay in delivery outrageous."*

- Salesperson: *"I see, you would like it at the originally agreed upon time."*

Whether used as a question or a statement, reframing needs to be used with a lot of tact in situations where there are a lot of negative emotions involved. If you overdo it and your reframing is too positive in relation to the very negative emotion of the customer, you often even intensify the negative emotion and thus make the situation worse.

- Customer (angry): *"Your service is lousy."*
  Salesperson: *"So you think we have a little potential for improvement?"*
  Customer (even angrier): *"A LITTLE POTENTIAL FOR IMPROVEMENT??? - That's the understatement of the century!"*

Used in this way, the reframing is placed too early and is too much of a good thing.

Negative reframing

However, reframing is a versatile tool that can be used not only to transform negative emotions or words into positive ones but also to reinforce slightly negative initial situations or even to transform positive situations and expressions into negative ones. Why would you want to do that? Wouldn't we rather have the customer in a positive mood or wouldn't we rather have him use words and expressions with positive connotations?

It depends on what your goal is. If, for example, you want to make the customer more aware of his problems or make him aware of them in the first place, you can also do this with the help of reframing.

An example situation with a young man who was a participant in one of my seminars and was selling equipment for saunas at the customer's site in direct sales:

- Me: *"Interesting business you're doing. What I'd be interested to know is what your closing ratio is on that. In how many cases do you sell something?"*
- Participant: *"I'm always selling!"*
- Me: *"As usual?"*
- Participant: *"Well, always."*
- Me: *"Wow. Do you know you have a problem?"* (reframing in a problem question)
- Participant (irritated): "*Why, I'm selling!?"*
- Me: *"Yeah, I do, but you're too cheap if you never lose a deal because of price."*

Of course, I could have made the participant aware of his problem, which he didn't even know about, in a different way. But by asking a question, it was probably more effective and more impactful. How can you use this type of question in sales?

- Customer: *"Production is **not** running **as smoothly as** it should in this area."*
  Salesperson: *"What exactly is the **problem**?"*

- Customer: *"Your competitor has also submitted a bid, but he's **a little slow** on delivery."*
  Salesman: *"How much **late** would he be?"*

- Customer: *"Our old heater is a **little too weak** on very cold days."*
  Salesman: *"That means when it's minus 10 degrees outside, your wife **freezes** in the living room?"*

The idea behind it is always the same: to reinterpret the customer's words more negatively by means of meaning reframing and thus - perceived - to increase the customer's problem.

Rhetorical questions

This type of question is probably one of the best known. Rhetorical questions are those to which the questioner does not expect an answer - which does not mean that your customer cannot answer them or sometimes does. But if the questioner does not expect an answer, why should this type of question be asked in conversations at all, and how can it be used to promote sales?

Such questions serve several purposes in sales. They are a stylistic device that makes the question seem almost like an assertion. Here are a few examples of questions and the statements hidden in them:

- Question: *"Haven't you already thought about it?"* - Assertion: *"You have already thought about it!"*

- Question: *"Doesn't that sound exciting?"* - Assertion: *"It sounds exciting!"*
- Question: *"Let me ask you directly: Who still believes such a thing?"* - Assertion: *"Nobody believes that anymore!"*
- Question: *"Have you also asked yourself if there is not a better solution?"* - Assertion: *"You have asked yourself that and there is a better solution."*
- *Question: "Don't we all want that?"* - Assertion: *"Everyone wants that!"*
- Question: *"What is it that makes this product so unique?"* - Assertion: *"The product is unique!"*

However, a question is a "softer" linguistic expression compared to an assertion. Statements such as *"Surely you've already thought about that!" are* much more likely to elicit resistance from the customer than the question variant.

With rhetorical questions, you can also influence subliminally and indirectly by packaging assertions as facts in the question without questioning them. The question *"Can you imagine that many customers are enthusiastic about this solution?" is* superficially about whether the customer can imagine that. In the background, however, it is simply asserted that many customers are enthusiastic.

So you suggest an assertion by communicating it in a way that is imperceptible to the conscious mind of your customer. You will learn much more about suggestions in the form of suggestive questions a little later. The boundaries between rhetorical and suggestive questions are often blurred. Because of this potentially suggestive effect of rhetorical questions, you should use them with great sensitivity.

The assertion as a question

One can further enhance the assertive effect of a rhetorical question by making a very clear assertion a rhetorical question by adding an attached "or."

- *"It's common knowledge that the effects of this compound are impressive, isn't it?"*
- *"You're also wondering how to solve this problem, aren't you?"*

This weakens the statement a bit, but at the same time, makes it easier to accept, because it is dressed up in the cloak of a question ... at least for the sake of form. Of course, one can discuss whether this is still a real question at all - according to the effect not, according to the form yes. Decide for yourself whether or where you want to use this potentially strongly influencing variant.

The break makes the difference

The formulation of a question as a rhetorical one is not solely determined by the wording itself, but also by the context and the way in which it is presented. These factors can influence whether the other person feels obliged to respond or recognizes that no answer is actually required.

In a lecture, for example, almost every question seems rhetorical. With an audience of 500, hardly anyone feels compelled to respond to a question posed by the speaker on stage. *"Do you really believe that's the truth?"*, for example, is tacitly understood by the audience as "*Everyone knows today that's not the truth."* In a one-on-one sales meeting, on the other hand, the same question might elicit a response from the customer.

Whether this is the case also depends greatly on whether you pause briefly after the question and give the customer time to give an answer, or continue speaking immediately (as if making a statement). If you also look at the customer expectantly during the pause, this reinforces the request for an answer.

Feedback questions

I could also describe feedback questions as a variant of rhetorical questions. They do not require an answer and - in case of an answer - would not result in a significant increase of information.

The classic feedback question goes something like this:

- *"So, if I understand you correctly, you mean that ...?"*
- *"Did I understand this correctly, that you ...?"*

Basically, you simply repeat what the customer said in a similar form (by paraphrasing/paraphrasing) or - usually even better - verbatim.

But even if you do not provide any additional or new information, feedback questions still fulfill some essential functions in the sales conversation:

- Use feedback questions to ensure the accuracy of a piece of information and reduce misunderstandings.
- In this way, you signal to the customer that you are listening to him and have understood him.
- In turn, you build or strengthen a relationship with the customer.

Feedback questions are an important part of active listening, which we discussed earlier in the book.

Scale issues

Scale questions are best used wherever you want to make the customer's answers more concrete and clear. You can therefore use them very well in addition to or in combination with concretization questions. With a scale question, you give the customer a scale on which to rate his answer.

A couple of examples:

- *"When you look at all your goals, on a scale of 1 - 10, how important is it to you to achieve this one specifically?"*
- *"On a scale of -100 to +100, how has your well-being changed in the past 12 months?"*

Scale questions are always very practical when there is no standardized way of evaluating. For example, when it comes to your customer's sales development, you don't necessarily need to use a scale question, because sales are always expressed in euros or percentages (when it comes to growth or even decline) anyway.

Scale questions are not only practical when the customer cannot give a simple, clear answer, but also when the customer does not want to or is not allowed to do so.

- *"If you rank your financial situation on a point scale of 1 - 5 points, how many points against you?"*
- *"What is the likelihood, as a percentage of 0 - 100 percent, that you will award the contract to us?"*

The scales can sometimes be very simple and rough. This makes it easier for the customer to give any answer.

- *"Just to get an indication. How much are we above the competition? Are we talking up to five percent or over five percent?"* (A simple scale question like this can help in the price discussion if the customer doesn't want to name the exact price of the competitor's offers).

So you see, scales in question form can be worked with very well in combination with many other types of questions. They are very practical and can be used well in a wide variety of areas in sales.

Leading questions

Leading questions have a bad reputation for "manipulation" in sales. And it is true. With an effective leading question, you can influence your counterpart without them noticing. But isn't "influencing" one of the essential goals of sales and marketing? In fact, I would argue that if a salesperson doesn't want to influence their customers in a certain direction, they are in the wrong job. After all, the goal of a sales conversation or process is to get the customer to buy. And suggestive questions can be very helpful in this.

Suggestion and manipulation are everywhere

This covert influence is even something quite commonplace. We find it packaged in multimedia form in every advertising message: images, smells, sounds, music and words influence us permanently.

When you smile nicely at the saleswoman in the bakery, you literally "force" her to smile back. Unconsciously and automatically. You have manipulated her suggestively, I could - strictly speaking - claim. You often ask suggestive questions yourself, without noticing it, as you will discover when you read on.

Paul Watzlawick, one of the great communication scientists, coined the famous saying:

"You can't not communicate!"

Every communication influences everyone who is involved. Wanted or not wanted. Consciously or unconsciously. Even when you say nothing, you influence. Think back to how you felt the last time you were silenced. So it is clear: No matter how you behave:

"You can't not influence."

Whether the influence we always exert in this way is based on a good or bad intention depends on the communicator, i.e. on you. If you use your influence to help your customers make a good buying decision or to make them smile (which I assume you do), there is nothing at all to stop you from using suggestive questions for this purpose, in my view.

What is a suggestion?

In order to understand suggestive questions well and to be able to use them correctly, we must first briefly deal with the concept of suggestion. What is suggestion? Suggestion is the influencing of an idea or sensation in a way that is not consciously perceived by the person being influenced. A suggestive question (and the messages hidden in it) works unconsciously, so to speak. This means that the conscious mind cannot act as a control instance because it is not aware of the influence.

A suggestive question is a question wrapped in a suggestion. Psychological questions of this type are also particularly effective because we tend to assume suggestions in statements rather than in questions.

Do NOT use leading questions here

You should, therefore, always NOT use a leading question in sales and marketing if you want an answer that is as uninfluenced as possible:

- In needs assessment or needs analysis, for example, suggestive questions are usually out of place (although there are exceptions).
- In market research or opinion polling surveys, it is a challenging task to formulate a questionnaire in such

a way that the questions are not suggestive and distort the results in a certain direction.

You will shortly find that in many situations, it is not at all easy NOT to put suggestions into questions and NOT to influence them by a question (quite strictly speaking, it is probably not possible at all).

Suggestive questions used perfectly

Suggestive questions, on the other hand, are perfect for many situations in sales pitches and marketing,

- to steer the conversation in the right direction that you want,
- to get answers you want to hear,
- to influence the thinking of your counterpart.

In the sales conversation, this type of question fits very well in

- the relationship building,
- the needs assessment (in special cases),
- in the offer presentation as intermediate questions,
- in the sales closing as closing questions,
- in dealing with objections (especially price objections),
- in the case of complaints than questions about complaint management.

Examples of the use of leading questions in all these situations can be found in the second part of the book.

4 Types of suggestive questions

There are a number of variations on how you can use or formulate suggestive questions. Not all of them are equally effective.

Variant #1 - The "flat" suggestive question

- *"**You agree that** this is the best decision you can make, right?"*

This type of question is one of the reasons why leading questions have a bad reputation. Strictly speaking, it is not a question, but a statement that only becomes a question through the appended *"or"*. It could also be called a rhetorical question, since the answer is only a formality and not expected at all.

It is too direct, too flat. The intention to influence in the form of an insinuation is too easy to see through. The customer notices it very quickly and is disgruntled.

In court, opposing counsel responds to this line of questioning quite quickly with the objection, *"Objection, leading question!"* Rightly so. These types of questions are best not used at all in professional sales communication, or only in isolated cases for very specific reasons.

Variant #2 - Suggestive questions as open questions

Suggestive questions can be packaged very well into open-ended questions.

- *"How* ***well do*** *you like my proposal?"*

In fact, in this way of asking, the suggestion is not immediately recognizable as such. In this example, the little word "good" is the suggestion. Thus, the questioner implies that the suggestion is "well" liked. So the question is not "if" the suggestion is liked, but only "how well". "Bad" is not completely ruled out as an answer, but it is less likely.

Whether questions harbor dangers in certain sales situations, in appointment acquisition, for example. After all, the customer could also answer "No" to the question "*Can we meet so I can show you our product? The* openly suggestive question *"When do we want to meet?"* will also not always, but much more often, lead to the desired result.

With this variant of an open question, you induce your counterpart to think in a certain direction and to exclude other directions of thought from the outset. Therefore, instead of asking IF, it is better to ask WHEN, WHO, HOW, HOW LONG, HOW OFTEN, etc., and you will significantly increase your chances of getting the answer you want.

The advantages of phrasing leading questions as open-ended questions are many:

- The suggestion is well hidden and the respondent is not aware of it (often not even the questioner).

- The respondent has the feeling of being able to answer completely freely and uninfluenced.
- You lead or direct the conversation without appearing dominant.

When you formulate suggestive questions, you build presuppositions into the questions. You assume or presuppose something specific.

A few examples of how you can formulate or use leading questions as open-ended questions in sales conversations:

- *"When do you want to decide?"* (The assumption here is that the customer wants to decide at all. It's just a matter of "when.")
- *"From your point of view, what are the advantages of our offer*?" (Assumption: It has advantages.)
- *"How well is business going*?" (Can be used in small talk/relationship building. Assumption: They are going well).
- *"Who else has to agree*?" (Assumption: The customer cannot decide alone.)
- *"How can we solve this*?" (Assumption: It can be solved by us).
- *"What do we have to do to get the job*?" (Assumption: We can get it.)
- *"When should we deliver*?" (Can be used as a closing question in a sales conversation. Assumption: We will receive the order).

- *"How do you want to pay?"* (As a closing question in sales. Assumption: The customer buys).
- *"What else do you need in addition?"* (As a question type in additional sales. Assumption: The customer buys something additional).

Variant #3 - Suggestive questions as closed questions

Suggestive questions can also be formulated in closed question form.

- *"Have you noticed how extremely soft and cuddly the material is?"*

If you want to formulate a closed question as a suggestive question, the principle is the same as for open questions. You build the suggestive wording, your message, into the question in such a way that it no longer appears to be in question, but a fixed given.

In our example, the suggestive phrase *"extremely soft and cuddly"*. The closed question refers to a different point, namely *"whether it was noticed"*.

Thus, suggestive questions can be phrased as open and closed questions, but the suggestion in the question wording is more transparent as a closed question and therefore, potentially less effective.

If an interlocutor sees through a suggestive question and recognizes the manipulative intent, it may have a negative effect on the rest of the conversation.

Therefore, when you ask suggestive questions, do it tactfully and not with a sledgehammer and formulate them as open questions. Also, if you do not want to hear no as an answer, then it is better to ask open questions and not OB (as already explained), which corresponds to a closed question.

Nevertheless, a few examples of suggestive questions in the form of closed questions:

- *"Have you had a chance to see the high quality for yourself?"* (As a type of question in the product presentation. Assumption: The quality is high).
- *"Do you want to book the coaching as well as the training?"* (As a closing question in sales. Assumption: He books the training).
- *"Can you imagine recommending our product, which you yourself like to use?"* (As a recommendation question. Assumption: He likes to use the product).
- *"Do you want to pay cash*?" (As a question in the sales closing before the yes to purchase has been explicitly said. Assumption: he will buy).

Variant #4 - Suggestive questions as alternative questions

Last but not least, suggestive questions can also be formulated as alternative questions.

- *"Do you want the four-pack of batteries or would you rather get the less expensive 12-pack?"*

Alternative formulations are even extremely well suited for suggestive questions. The principle of formulating suggestive questions as alternative questions works as follows: You only pack answer alternatives into the question that are okay for you or desirable as an answer. In this way, you give your counterpart the choice between "good" and "very good.

Remember the example with the breakfast eggs in the chapter on alternative questions? This type of suggestive questioning - as studies show time and again - immediately sells more.

A few examples of the use of alternative suggestive questions in sales:

- *"Do you want the pack of five or would you prefer the advantageous promotional pack of 20?"* (A closing question formulated suggestively. Assumption: He wants at least the five-pack).
- *"Should the device have a larger or smaller display?"* (An alternative question as a demand question. Assumption: devices without a display are out of the question).
- *"Should we deliver this week or early next?"* (An alternative question as a closing question. Assumption: The customer buys and we should deliver).

As you can see, alternative questions can develop their suggestive power particularly well as closing questions.

In summary, suggestive questions are a very powerful type of question in sales psychology. You can use them very effectively in many situations and achieve very good results with them.

The decisive factor here is ...

- the right question
- at the appropriate time
- to the right interlocutor
- in the right form, i.e. with the necessary tact, and
- with "honorable" intent.

Under these conditions, it is also absolutely okay to use such effective instruments of manipulation through language as leading questions in sales conversations.

Proposal questions

Sometimes the situation in a sales conversation may also require making suggestions instead of asking questions. It can speed up the flow of the conversation, especially when the customer still knows too little to give a meaningful answer to an open-ended question such as, *"What is important to you about your new windows?"*

In such situations, you can work either with closed questions or also with alternative questions:

- *"Do you want triple glazing for better sound insulation?"* (Closed question)
- *"Do you want double glazing on your windows or triple for even better insulation?"* (Alternative question)

In principle, suggestions are already packed into the question here by giving you the alternatives to choose from. With the suggestion question, you go one step further and package the suggestions that you think make sense as follows:

- *"What do you think about going with triple glazing to have it even quieter in the living room?"*
- *"I recommend triple glazing for even more peace and quiet indoors. What do you think about it?"*
- *"Have you also thought about opting for triple glazing to keep out even more street noise?"* (In this variant, the suggestion is packaged very indirectly in a closed question).

When you work with these types of questions, you get less of your customer's uninfluenced opinion or even ideas, but you increase the chance that the suggestions and ideas you recommend or prefer will be accepted by the customer.

Among other things, this type of question is also helpful and well-applicable in complaint situations, which we will discuss in great detail in the second part of the book.

- *"What do you say we send someone over today to take a look at the problem?"*

Wherever you could or normally would make suggestions, you might as well wrap those suggestions up in a question. In this way, you give your counterpart the feeling that he or she has the choice and makes the decision, although you naturally limit this choice by asking in this way and influencing the decision in the desired direction.

Wordless questions

Questions do not always have to be put into words. In various sales situations, you can also ask questions wordlessly and your counterpart will still understand the questions because it arises from the situation and what has been said before. To phrase a question in body language, you need to do the following:

- Maintain eye contact with the customer,
- Hold palms turned upward at about belly level,
- Raise your eyebrows and make a questioning expression.

Then you only need to wait for the customer's response.

This way of asking questions can only be used very selectively. Only when it is clear from the context what is being asked will the question be understood. Without the appropriate context, it does not work. At the same time, it can be a very interesting variant, even in difficult sales phases such as price discussions or more generally in objection handling:

- Customer: *"That's quite a lot you want for that front door."*
  The salesman asks without a word.
  Customer: *"Of course, I realize that this is the top model.*
  Seller asks wordlessly.
  Customer: *"And quality has its price, of course."*

If you use wordless questions in this way when dealing with objections, the customer may begin to make their own case in response to your question, which would normally be made by the salesperson.

Target questions

In sales processes or discussions, it is helpful for the salesperson to know what the customer's goal or goals are. By asking target questions, the customer is prompted to think about his goals. If he has not already done so, this can trigger a thoroughly lengthy thought process. In this way, not only does the salesperson learn something about the customer's goals, but the customer may also gain more clarity about his goals in a particular area, if he did not already have them.

A few examples of target questions:

- *"What exactly do you want to achieve with this project?"* (A target question in combination with a concretization question)
- *"What is your desired weight?"*
- *"What are you trying to do?"*
- *"What do you want your employees to be able to do after the seminar?"*
- *"How exactly will you know you've reached your goal?"*
- *"What needs to happen for you to be satisfied with the outcome?"*

- *"Do you want your target return on investment to be over five percent?"* (Target questions can also be formulated in closed form).
- *"Is it more important to you to get to your destination as quickly as possible, or do you want to enjoy the ride to the maximum?"* (An alternative destination question)

The salesperson acts like a coach, so to speak, by asking target questions. By "forcing" the customer with such questions to be as clear as possible about what he wants to achieve, he improves the chances of achieving exactly that for the customer. This is also an important element in almost every coaching conversation. On closer inspection - and not just with target questions - a good sales conversation has a lot in common with a good coaching conversation.

Often, the customer's initial answers to target questions will still be vague and fuzzy, especially if they have not yet thought about the goals. Then, as a salesperson, you can follow up with concretization questions to get even more clarity.

- *"What exactly does more success mean to you?"*
- *"What exactly do you measure the success of this measure by?"*
- *"What exactly will be different when the project is complete?"*
- *"When you say you want to get fitter, what exactly will you be able to accomplish as a fit person?"*

If, through your questions, you manage not only to formulate the customer's goal more clearly, but perhaps even to install a kind of goal image in the customer's mind, then this is even better and more effective - due to the stronger emotional effect of images. The goal then develops a stronger pull effect.

- *"If you imagine what it will be like to have achieved your goal - more fitness - what will that be like?"*
- *"Assuming you have achieved your goal, how will you feel*?" (An emotional, hypothetical goal question)

By asking further, you can also bring other sensory channels into the target picture and thus even put the customer in a comprehensive target state. Let's stay with the fitness goal example for a moment. Here it could read like this:

- *"What will you look like?"*
- *"What are you going to say?"*
- *"How will your body feel?"*
- *"What will others say about you?"* (A circular target question - we'll get to that in a moment).
- *"What will your husband/wife say to you?"* (A circular target question)
- *"What will you say to yourself?"*

Are these still questions you can use in sales, you may ask. Well, it all depends on what you are selling. If someone is selling perforated sheets to industrial companies, such questions would probably go too far. For a personal trainer who wants to sell a program for the dream body, such questions are exactly the tools that will help him not only to convince prospects, but to inspire them. But that doesn't mean that our perforated sheet salesperson can't and won't ask the simple target question "*What do you want to achieve by using these new perforated sheets* in your *product?" to* the buyer in the industrial company and also get an answer.

Circular questions

We often see the world too one-sidedly, only from our point of view. While this is an important perspective, it is not the only one from which one should view the world in sales. Putting yourself in the customer's shoes and looking at the offer from their eyes, for example, can already bring very interesting insights. Although this is highly recommended, it is far from all the different perspectives you can use in sales.

With circular questions, you get the customer to look at something - an offer, a product, a procedure, a solution, or even the current situation - from different perspectives. The main focus here is on the perspectives of the relevant people in your customer's environment. Depending on the industry or offer, this can be the family members, the partner, the supervisor, the customers, the colleagues, the suppliers, the neighbors etc.

To make it clearer what kind of questions we are now talking about, a few examples of circular questions. Often these are hypothetical and/or directed into the future:

- *"When you pull up at home in your new car, how will your wife react?"*
- *"What would your boss think of you if you implemented this as discussed from now on?"*

But these simple circular questions by no means exhaust the full potential of this questioning technique for sales. You can also ask questions with a little more variation and, in the process, get the customer to think around a corner or even two:

- *"How would you argue in my place to convince you?"* This is certainly a question (e.g., for objection handling) that your counterpart will most likely have to think about a bit. Asking questions in the sales conversation that the customer didn't expect and will have to think about how to answer is beneficial.
- *"If you were to travel ten years into the future and ask your future self about it, what would he advise you to do?"*
Admittedly, this is a somewhat exotic variant of a circular question, but it shows that it doesn't always have to be other people whose points of view you can use. It can also be past or future variations of your customer and their points of view.
- *"How would Donald Trump view this problem?"* You can also use people who are well-known without your client having to know them personally.
- *"What would Steve Jobs advise you in this regard?"* These people don't even have to live anymore.
- *"What tips would Apple give you regarding your current situation?"*
It can also be companies, organizations (the Catholic Church) or states (the USA) whose glasses they put on the customer by means of a circular question.

You can ask these more exotic questions, especially if the relationship with the customer is very good, he trusts you even if you ask strange questions, and if they fit the situation.

At the same time, circular questions do not have to be hypothetical; they can be asked more directly.

- *"How will your neighbors react to the new pool?"* By using "will" instead of "would", you build a pre-assumption - the customer will buy the pool - into the question, or subliminally suggest that they should accept your offer.
- *"How does your partner see the current housing situation?"*
  These questions can be used very well - in needs assessment, for example - not only for future situations, but also for present ones, in order to know the needs of all concerned.
- *"What is important to your customers in relation to this product?"*
- *"What did your suppliers say about you in the last survey?"* (Circular questions can also refer to the past).

Circular questions can serve the following functions in sales conversations:

- By making the customer think about something from new angles, they bring new insights to light (for the salesperson as well as for the customer).
- Above all, they are also an important variant of ecology issues and help to ensure that the customer's

relevant environment also reacts positively to the customer's purchase decision. Why is this important? Not least for reducing the cancellation rate. If your customer buys something and, for example, his wife gives him hell about it at home, he may not only regret his purchase but also withdraw from it.

- They facilitate understanding for others or even between you and your customer, for example, when you ask the question, *"What would you do if you were me?"*
- By showing new perspectives, they help to bring movement into deadlocked discussion situations.

All in all, circular questions are very practical tools for various situations in customer contact, especially because - in my opinion - they are used relatively little and can therefore have a stronger effect because your customer does not know them and does not expect them that way.

A small request

We have now completed the first part of the book. I hope there is already one or two things in it that you can put to good use in your sales practice. Ideally, you have even already done so successfully. In that case, I especially congratulate you. Basically, it would even be enough if you have successfully used just one point, one questioning technique from the book, once. That alone will probably have won you more than you invested in the book. That's the advantage of good sales books: they pay for themselves very quickly and easily.

As an author, it's important for me to know how my readers like the book. Based on reader comments, I am always revising my books to make them more substantive and practical. So if you want to contribute an additional idea from your practice, just send me an email at service@romankmenta.com.

And, of course, you would help me a lot if you also leave a review on Amazon or the platform where you purchased the book. Would you do that for me? - If so, either do it now if you think you've already read enough to write a short review. Of course, if you want to finish reading the book before writing your review, I'd be just as happy. In any case, thank you very much for this!

Why am I writing this request now and not at the end of the book? Experience shows that something like this is quickly overlooked at the very end. And now: Be curious about the second part.

PART 2:

AREAS OF APPLICATION OF QUESTIONS IN SALES AND CUSTOMER CONTACT

After we have looked at a number of very useful questioning techniques for your sales conversations in the first part of the book, we will check them in the second part for their applicability in different situations with customer contact. These are mainly phases in sales conversations themselves. But even before or after the actual sales talk, at the end of which the customer hopefully buys, there are situations with customer contact - such as appointment acquisition or a complaint - in which questions are an important lever for success.

I have arranged all these situations in the second part along the sales process or sales talk to give it a logical and comprehensible structure.

We will cover the following situations:

- Telephone appointment acquisition,
- Relationship building,
- First-time customer contact in retail,
- Needs assessment/needs analysis,

- Demand generation,
- Presentation,
- Objection Handling,
- Price negotiation,
- Graduation,
- Upselling,
- Cross-selling/additional sales,
- Customer loyalty,
- Complaints and grievances.

In the individual situations, you will then find a number - sometimes a large number - of examples of questions that can be optimally used for them. Sometimes these questions will be formulated in such a way that you can adopt and use them 1:1. Sometimes, you will feel you need to rephrase them. Do that because the wording should match your usage. As long as the basic idea behind a question remains intact, this is the best course of action.

You won't find every question type in every situation below, but you will find many of them in most. The point is not to accommodate every question type in every situation by hook or by crook (although you certainly could), but rather to have optimally suited examples of use that you can incorporate into your practice.

The order is crucial

Imagine a young man approaching a young woman he doesn't know at the bar in the evening and the first question he asks her is, *"Tell me, are children on your life plan?"* How do you think she would react? My guess is that this could well be where the contact ends. But that doesn't mean that the question itself is an inappropriate one, or one that he generally shouldn't ask. But - and this is crucial - it is in the wrong place here. It was clearly asked too early.

It is the same in sales. You may or should even ask all questions whose answers are important for you or the customer. The only thing you should pay attention to is the order. Not every question is suitable or appropriate at every point. There are questions that concern sensitive areas (often topics such as health, finances, or relationships) that should not be asked at the beginning of a sales contact. Later on, however, when the relationship with the customer has been established and trust has been built up, you can not only ask such questions, but you will even get answers to them if you have proceeded with tact.

Appointment acquisition by phone

Contacting potential customers, who are not yet known, by telephone - also referred to as cold calling - with the purpose of setting up an appointment is almost like an art form. Even experienced salespeople find this activity to be one of the most challenging in sales. The strategies to succeed at it are plentiful and can fill up several books.

Questions are particularly exciting in this context because they help you to successfully circumvent or even master certain critical points. In the following paragraphs, you will therefore not receive a complete strategy for telephone appointment acquisition, but a "best of" tips and small psychological tricks in question form.

In the anteroom

Depending on the size of the company you are calling, you may first end up at the reception or with an assistant of your target person. This "hurdle" must first be overcome in order to be put through. There, you will hear the following question quite often: *"What is this about?"* If you now answer what it is about, it may well be that the person replies by return mail that this is not needed and the conversation already ends again at this point. Instead of answering, you can also ask a question at this point.

- Salesperson: *"Franz Mustermann please."*
  Assistant: *"What is it about, if you don't mind me asking?"*
  Salesperson: *"Ah, isn't he back from lunch yet?"* - (A counter question instead of an answer returns control in the conversation. He who asks, leads).
  Assistant: *"He should be here in a few minutes."* Salesman: *"Fine, then I'll get right back to you."* 15 minutes later. Salesperson: *"We spoke on the phone a few minutes ago. Would you be so kind as to put me through to Franz Mustermann!"* - (At this point, DO NOT ask a question, but give an order, lowering your voice at the end).
  Assistant: *"Yes, I'd be happy to."*

Can this be done in a completely different way? Sure! Can it be that the assistant insists on knowing what it's all about? Of course! But you have significantly improved the chances that it will go something like this or something similar to the above by asking a counter question.

At the target

If you have successfully mastered the "anteroom hurdle" or even directly if there is none, you end up with the target person. Your conversation partner on the other end of the line does not know you and has several questions in mind at once:

- *"Who is that?"*
- *"Why should I listen to him?"*
- *"What does he want?"*
- *"What's in it for me?"*
- *"How long does it take?"*

As hard as it sounds, very often, his first impulse will be to want to get rid of you as soon as possible. Many salespeople jump in awkwardly and start texting the potential customer with endless statements about how great their offer is. The customer will take the first opportunity - when the salesperson needs to take a breath - to tell the salesperson that he or she has no need ... for whatever.

It would be much nicer to get a yes instead of a no right at the start, wouldn't it? And that's what you get with the following question:

- *"Dear Mr. Mustermann, I know your time is limited. May I therefore get straight to the point?"*

Hardly any customer will answer no here. And strengthened by an initial agreement, the conversation is easier to continue. In addition, you signal to the customer that you consider his time valuable and that it will go quickly.

The conversation with the target person is in many respects like a - very short - sales pitch, in which you can use all kinds of question types. It can be particularly helpful to ask problem questions to find out where the shoe pinches.

- *"Mr. Mustermann, you just said that you are directly affected by the legal change. May I ask in what way?"*

Following this, it naturally lends itself to asking solution questions (mostly hypothetical):

- *"You just said that the change in the law means you have to make higher provisions. If I had an interesting solution for that, would that be worth 30 minutes of your time?"*

This question is perfect if you want to filter out on the phone with whom an appointment makes sense and where such an appointment would be rather a waste of time. If you absolutely want to make an appointment, then you should work with a suggestive question and instead of asking about the IF of an appointment, always ask about its WHEN.

- *"When is a good time for you?"*
- *"When can we see each other?"*

- *"I'll be in your area on the 10th of the month. When is convenient for you?"* - (The "Am in the area" variant works very well for appointments).

This way of asking - or better: the basic idea behind it - is probably one of the most important points in telephone appointment acquisition at all. It is a completely different view of the world if you, as a salesperson, assume that you will get an appointment in any case and the only question is when it will be.

To determine the exact date, you could, of course, make suggestions, which you formulate as open or even closed questions. This works, of course, but it has its pitfalls. Even if the customer has agreed in principle to an appointment, he may still be a shaky candidate who could still change his mind.

- Salesperson: *"What does Monday at 3 p.m. look like?"*
  Customer: *"I'm afraid I can't do that."*
  Salesperson: *"And Tuesday at 9 a.m.?"*
  Customer: *"I'm scheduled for that, too."*
  Salesperson: *"And on Thursday at 2 p.m.?"*
  Customer: *"I'm sorry, but I can't do it then either. You know what, we'll do it differently. You send me something and then we'll talk on the phone again."*

Of course, you could also ask quite openly, *"When is a good time for you?" In* many cases, this will also work without any problems. However, I have often experienced that customers were somewhat overwhelmed.

To avoid a situation like the one above, you can work with the so-called appointment funnel. Instead of making appointment suggestions to the customer, you ask him alternative questions with which you steer him in the desired direction, but without being too directive. The customer selects an appointment himself and you have your appointment.

- Salesperson: *"Would you prefer that we meet this week or better next?"*
  Customer: *"Better next week, this one is already quite full."*
  Salesperson: *"First or second half of the week?"*
  Customer: *"The second one is quieter with me."*
  Salesperson: *"Do you prefer Thursday or Friday?"*
  Customer: *"Friday would be good."*
  Salesperson: *"Morning or afternoon?"*
  Customer: *"In the afternoon we finish early."*
  Salesman: *"So that means in the morning. Right at 9 a.m. or would you prefer 11 a.m.?"*
  Customer: *"11 o'clock fits well."*
  Salesman: *"So that means I'll be at your place next Friday at 11 am. It's on the books. I'm looking forward to it."*

Does this seem a bit complicated to you? Maybe, but it is a very safe way to the appointment, where you always keep the conversation in your hands and the customer can no longer "run away" from you.

Relationship building

During the first contact with your customer, the course is set on the relationship level. In most sales situations, there is one goal above all: to appear likeable and competent. In the first few minutes, your customer decides - usually unconsciously - whether he likes you and considers you competent.

Now there are salespeople who have a strong sense of mission and use the initial contact to impress the customer right from the start with how great their company, their products, and of course, they themselves are. In the rarest of cases, this creates a feeling of sympathy in the counterpart.

It is quite different if you simply ask questions and listen. At the beginning, it is not yet about the reason for the conversation, but about very general, uncomplicated and harmless topics. However, you should not leave the start of the conversation to chance. You should also think about what questions you can ask in advance.

The classics are questions like, *"How are you?"* You can already ask these if you can't think of anything else. But there are more opportunities, especially in corporate business (B2B), because appointments are made in advance and you find out about your customer and their company online beforehand. A short online research will tell you a lot about the company you are dealing with, which you can also use for good small talk questions to build the relationship, if necessary.

Or you may see something on the company premises or while you are perhaps waiting that you can use as a hook for questions. With more "unusual" questions, you can out yourself as someone who opens his eyes and ears and shows interest. At the same time, however, these questions must not be "indiscreet," since you are still very early in the interview process. To avoid the risk of appearing "indiscreet," you can either include a question allowance in your question or warn that you may be indiscreet. You will read how to do this in a moment.

A few examples of relationship building questions:

- *"May I ask you what this interesting sculpture in the reception area represents?"* (A closed question with permission to ask)
- *"At the risk of being indiscreet, what is your handicap?"* (A question that may be appropriate when looking at a golf trophy).
- *"How are you getting along with the new Apple Watch?"*
- *"Can I ask - you have a Tesla parked out front - what's the range really like?"*
- *"What made you decide to move the whole company?"*
- *"I see you have the shirts custom made. May I ask where?"*

As you can see, the content of questions in relationship building can encompass anything, even small details that can be explored in depth. In most cases, simple, open-ended questions are sufficient (your customers are more likely to start talking than with closed questions). More sophisticated questioning techniques are usually not necessary at this point.

Retail entry question

A special situation is the initial contact in retail. This is different from classic B2B customer contact in that the salesperson here does not know who will be entering the store next and often does not know the customers. If a customer comes into the store, after a greeting, the salesperson should naturally try to make contact with them somehow and start a conversation.

"Is there anything I can do for you?" is usually all you get to hear as a customer. *"What can I do for you?",* phrased as an open question, is a little better, but far from being really good. Why? As a customer walking into a retail store, you know what you're going to hear, *"What can I do for you?"* And if, like many customers, you just want to take a look around, you already have the appropriate response prepared: *"Thanks, I just want to take a look around." At* this point, contact with the customer is already over. The customer takes a look around and often leaves the store again without any further interaction with the salesperson. A pity. Because, as you've probably experienced yourself, a good salesperson who manages to engage you in conversation can sell you something even when you might not have intended to buy anything.

The question now is, how can the salesperson engage with the customer without receiving an immediate rebuff? According to the idea of this book, the solution is, of course, to ask good questions. Or even better: ask surprising questions. Questions to which the customer does not have a standard answer that he automatically reels off.

A few examples of this, some of which you might find "exotic," but "exotic" often means effective in this sales situation:

- Salesperson: *"Excuse me, can I ask you something?"* Customer (surprised): *"Yes, please."* (The customer already says yes, which is a good start).
  Salesperson: *"We are currently considering painting the wall here a color and are wavering between this and this color* (salesperson shows the customer two color samples). *Which one do you like better?"*
  Customer: *"Mmmh. I think this one. The other one rather not so."*
  Salesman: *"Thank you. But you came for something else. What can I do for you?"*

  The likelihood that the customer will now reel off his *"Thanks, I just want to take a look around."* is significantly reduced after the surprise entrance and due to the fact that you have already exchanged a few sentences and gotten to know each other a bit.

- Salesman: *"Good afternoon. Tell me, if you don't mind me asking, has that construction site up ahead been cleared by now?"*
  Customer: *"Yeah, I didn't see anything else."*
  Salesman: *"That means you got here all right?"* Customer: *"Yes, fine."*
  Salesperson: *"And what brought you here?"*

  What was said in the previous example applies. The chances of real communication with the customer have improved.

- Saleswoman (asks male customer): *"Sorry, I'm a little embarrassed. But this box is so heavy and you are clearly stronger than I am* (a small compliment, accompanied by a smile, doesn't hurt). *Would you lift the box for me here on the table?"*
  Customer (surprised): *"Yeah sure, I'd be happy to."* (Lifts the box onto the table)
  Saleswoman: *"Thank you very much. You've been very helpful. But I guess you didn't come to us because you are looking for a job as a warehouse worker* (smiling). *What can I do for YOU?"*

  Again, communication is likely to continue. What has an additional positive effect here is that asking someone for a small favor makes us sympathetic. With the next customer, the saleswoman might ask the same question, only then it's about moving the box down from the table.

- Customer is standing by a shelf with a product in hand. For example, the salesperson might ask the following questions without any warning at all:
  - *"What do you like about it?"* (Open, suggestive question)
  - *"How does it feel?"* (Open, emotional questions)
  - *"Would you give something like that away?"*
  - *"How would someone react if you gave this to them?"* (Open, circular question)
  - *"Who do you think this product would be most suitable for as a gift?"*

- *"How many points out of ten would you give this product?"* (scale question)
- *"Are you looking for something really expensive?"* (Closed, paradoxical question)
- *"Can you imagine using something like this?"* (Hypothetical question)
- *"This is often bought and often returned. Do you know why?"* (Closed, paradoxical question)

So be creative when you often have these special contact situations and come up with something different than the standard approach, because very often, you will only get the standard rejection. Ask surprising questions and you will be surprised how easily you can start a conversation with the customers.

Needs assessment

The needs assessment or needs analysis is probably the phase in a sales conversation that most people associate most readily with questions. And that is true. Questions - along with active listening - are the most important communicative tool in needs assessment. As a salesperson, you don't need to do more than ask good questions and listen professionally at this stage. However, after you may have to ask a lot of questions, especially if it is a product that has many options or/and the customer is not very talkative, it is important to ask very varied questions. In the context of needs assessment, you can probably use all the questioning techniques discussed in the first part of the book.

Question permission

As mentioned earlier, the order of the questions you ask is relevant. This is especially true for the needs assessment. As part of this, you will often ask straightforward questions, especially at the beginning of a sales call. But sometimes, in this phase, you will also ask or need to ask questions about points that your counterpart may not be comfortable talking about (more likely later in this phase).

At the beginning of the needs assessment, it is advisable to obtain permission to ask questions. This works quite simply by asking if you are allowed to ask questions:

- *"So I can be as specific as possible about what you need ... Is it okay if I ask you a few questions?"*

Ideally, you combine this question permission with a reason (in the example at the beginning of the question). This explains your question, introduces it, and increases the likelihood of agreement. In the vast majority of cases, you will get a yes answer. If a no comes at this point, you may have a deeper problem with your customer - probably at the relationship level. You might say that, sales-wise, asking permission is just a formality, a kind of rhetorical question. Yes, it is. And yet - if you initiate this phase of the conversation in this way - you can ask even more questions and go into even more depth without it seeming strange to the customer that you are asking so much.

Varied questions instead of interrogations

Speaking of strange, some salespeople's fear of asking too many questions is more than unfounded. In my practice as a customer, I have hardly ever experienced the feeling of being quizzed or "interrogated" by a salesperson. I regularly experience the opposite, that I am asked few or no questions at all.

If there is a risk that the customer feels questioned, then it is most likely to be in the needs assessment, as this is where the vast majority of questions are asked. But you can counteract this quite easily:

- Ask your questions in a varied way. Use different types of questions (you have enough choice in the first part of the book).
- Mix your questions with a little information. For some questions, it is necessary to include some information anyway, so that the customer can answer them reasonably.
    - *"This seat is available in two versions. On the one hand, the standard version, or on the other hand, the ventilated version with built-in air conditioning so you don't sweat. Which variant appeals to you more?"*

For very specific topics that the customer may not talk about with everyone or may be very reluctant to talk about, you can reiterate and reinforce the question permission for the individual case by additionally including objection anticipation (bold):

- *"May I ask you an* ***indiscreet, impertinent*** *... question?"*

Avoid chain questions

What I also observe time and again is that salespeople ask so-called chain questions in the heat of the moment. That means that instead of asking just one question and giving the customer time to answer, they ask two or sometimes three questions in a row and chain them together. The customer then usually only answers the last one.

Therefore, ask only one question at a time and wait for the answer before asking the next one. Moreover, the answer could also provide valuable information for the next question.

Questions about the product

Broadly speaking, the potential questions in the needs assessment can be divided into two areas:

- Questions that relate directly to the product or service, and
- Questions about the framework (about everything "around the product").

Let's start with the questions about the product. These are also the ones that most sellers (almost) always ask, as no offer can be made without the answers to them.

Examples include:

- *"Where exactly is the pain in your back?"* (Open question)
- *"What should the smartphone be able to do?"* (Open question)

- *"Do you want to have a fingerprint door opener?"* (Closed question)
- *"Do you like the coupe or the station wagon better?"* (Alternative question)
- *"There are three engine options: 155 hp, 210 hp or 300 hp. Which one do you want?"* (Alternative question)
- *"Do you want the seminar to last one or two days?"* (Alternative question)

These are the classic needs questions that must be asked in order to specify the product or service. In many cases, no offer can be made without this information anyway. That's why customers usually answer these questions quite easily.

The wording of these questions is often quite simple. They can also be used very well at the beginning of the needs analysis, since they usually do not touch on any sensitive topics and the customer usually has an answer ready quickly. I could also say that the customer and the salesperson use these questions to warm up.

Questions about the general conditions

At this point, general conditions is understood as a generic term for everything else that you can or should inquire about, but which is not directly related to the product or service. This can include the following topics:

- planned areas of application for the product,
- Objectives pursued with the product or service,

- Decision-making process and decision-makers,
- future plans,
- Finance and funding,
- previous purchasing decisions or suppliers,
- the (physical) environment in which the product is used or the service is provided, and
- everything that comes before or after the product or service (both physically and in timing).

Especially if you are selling to businesses, you can also ask the following:

- Company and business development (in the B2B sector),
- Corporate Structures/Organizational Charts,
- other projects that may be of interest to you.

Especially if you sell to private consumers, can be asked about it:

- Hobbies and preferences,
- Relationship status and marital status,
- Place of residence and lifestyle,
- Occupation.

Now, if you think that some of these topics go too far and have nothing to do with the actual purchase decision, let me show you a few examples of how crucial these topics can be.

Example private car purchase:

- **Question about relationship status and marital status**

If the customer is about to get married, his wife may already be pregnant or children are planned soon, which definitely impacts the size of the vehicle.

- **Residence and lifestyle**

If the customer lives in an apartment without a garage in the city centre, then slightly smaller models have the advantage for him that it is easier to find a parking space. But if he has a garage, then there are maximum dimensions for vehicles for it.

- **Hobbies and preferences**

When asked about this, it might turn out that the customer is generally someone who cares about ecology and sustainability. This is an important point when it comes to fuels (gasoline or diesel) or electric drive. Also, the consumption and the amount of recycled material built into the car can be arguments that benefit you and please the customer.

Example purchase of a machine for an industrial company:

- **Decision-makers and decision-making processes** This is an important topic to ask about in the private sector as well, but in B2B sales it is a must. Most of the time, there are several co-decision makers and influencers in major decisions. Finding out who all has a say and who has what influence will determine whether you close a deal or not.

- **Future plans**
  Finding out about your customer's future plans is also helpful for the current business. For example, suppose you ask whether your customer plans to buy another machine next year, but doesn't do so right away for budgetary reasons. In that case, you can include the purchase of another machine right away in any price negotiations.

- **Finance and financing**
  Knowing how your customer plans to finance the purchase can also yield interesting points to include when negotiating terms.

So you see, the more you know about the customer, the easier the sales pitch will be. Some of these topics are, as mentioned, not always easy to ask. But with the right questioning technique at the right time and with a portion of tact, you can literally ask anything.

Although, in principle, all question types from the first part of the book can be used for the needs assessment, a few of them deserve special attention again.

Requirement questions as a fixed part of the requirements survey

At the very beginning, it is almost always advisable to ask a requirement question that relates to the product:

- *"When you think about your new home, what is most important to you?"*

- *"When you think about booking a vacation, what do you look for most?"*
- *"You want to invest your inheritance, you said. What is important to you in this?"*

For more complex services that are geared towards a longer collaboration, it might also make sense to move the requirement question back a bit, as you might then get more open answers to it - but you should ask it in any case:

- *"When you select a consultant, what is most important to you about them?"*
- *"What would you value in our collaboration?"*
- *"If we work together, what would I have to do to make you happy?"*

In the answers to requirements questions, references to the product will always be intermixed with answers that refer to framework conditions. In practice, you will rarely or never find the sharp distinctions that I try to maintain here in the book. That is the case, and it doesn't matter.

Emotion-related questions for hidden information

Emotion-related issues are often neglected, especially in B2B sales. *"Emotions have no place in business,"* many think. This is precisely why emotion-related questions in the needs assessment can provide you with very valuable and otherwise hidden information about the customer and their motivations.

- *"What does your gut tell you when you think about swapping the machine?"*

- *"What keeps you up at night when you think about your sales department?"* (Emotion-related problem question)
- *"How do you feel about the thought of adding a new product of this type to your line?"*

Counter questions to keep the reins in your hand

Some customers want to know everything about the product or service very early in the conversation - especially during the needs assessment - and start asking questions themselves. They are perfectly entitled to do so, and the salesperson may or should, of course, also provide an answer. However, he must be careful not to maintain the pattern - customer asks, salesperson answers. He must get the reins back in his hand to lead the conversation. This works very well with a counter-question.

- Customer: *"Does this come in other sizes?"*
  Salesman: *"What size do you need?"*
- Customer: *"What excursions are offered during the stay?"*
  Salesperson: *"What are your preferences?"*
- Customer: *"Can you deliver earlier?"*
  Seller: *"When would be the ideal delivery time for you?"*

Hypothetical questions to expand thinking

Similar to emotion-related questions, hypothetical questions in the context of needs assessment help to expand the customer's thinking. In this way, they provide information that you would not get if you only asked about what is and not about what could be.

- *"If money were no object, which model would appeal to you?"*
- *"If you had more time, how would that affect your selection?"*
- *"If you could decide on your own, what would be most important to you?"* (Hypothetical requirement question)

Target questions to know where to go

Getting clarity on the customer's goals is an important part of the needs assessment process - for the customer and the salesperson alike. In the process, you might also discover that what the customer wants to achieve is not feasible with the solution they envision.

- *"What exactly are you trying to accomplish with this project?"*
- *"The perfect vacation, what does it look like for you?"* (Combined target and requirement question)
- *"When the project is complete and you look back on it, what did you accomplish?"* (Goal question that puts the customer in the future)

Feedback questions to signal understanding

In the needs assessment, the salesperson should ideally do only two things: ask good questions and listen excellently. Feedback questions are a part of listening that lets the customer know that you hear and understand what they are saying. This not only ensures that you correctly understand what is being said, but also strengthens the relationship.

- *"If I understand you correctly, timeliness of deliveries is extremely important to you?"*
- *"So you are saying that your windows must be very well insulated against sound. Did I understand that correctly?*

Problem questions to create pain

If your customer has problems and you have the solution, then that's good for you - as hard as that may sound. But it is also an advantage for the customer if you use problem questions to uncover the critical points in the needs analysis, make them aware of them, and perhaps even reinforce them. After all, you have a solution that helps the customer.

- *"What are you currently struggling with most when it comes to finding employees?"*
- *"What of what you've already tried to attract new customers hasn't worked?"*
- *"What have you wasted money on in the last few months trying to get your production bottlenecks under control?"*

It is best to ask additional questions with problem deepening questions to make the pain even more palpable.

- *"How does your crooked nose affect your life?" (The* plastic surgeon might ask.)

- *"Have you ever calculated how much extra heating costs are due to the fact that your home is not yet appropriately insulated?"*
- *"How much does it cost you to change a vendor when you factor in all the impacts?"*

Demand generation

However, by asking questions, you can analyze the customer's needs, survey the existing demand, and create additional demand. Your customer very often does not know,

- what all you have to offer (even if you have been working with him for years),
- what solutions already exist for its problems and
- which problems he doesn't even have yet, but could get, and what solutions there are for them.

This can sometimes go so far as to offer a solution to a problem you are "creating" in the first place. In medicine, it is said: *"There are no healthy people, only badly examined ones."* Similarly, in sales, it could be said, *"There are no customers without problems, just ones where the salespeople haven't asked the right questions yet."*

But it doesn't always have to be problems that create a need. Often, they are simply additional opportunities.

- Salesperson: *"Have you ever made desserts on your gas grill?"*
  Customer: *"Is it possible?"*
  Salesman: *"Yes, of course. Shall I show you how?"*

- Salesperson: *"Do you want the insurance to pay even if it's your own fault?"*
- Salesperson: *"Should we also make sure you not only get a great website, but also a lot of visitors?"*

Of course, you could also say what additional possibilities you or your product can offer the customer. However, making him curious (or testing his curiosity) by means of a question and then, because he wants to, telling him more about it is the much more elegant way.

Presentation

In a sales conversation, the product or offer presentation is the phase in which the salesperson naturally has a large - probably the largest - share of speech in the entire conversation. And not only that. The proportion of statements is also significantly greater here than the number of questions that are asked. As a result, there is a risk that the salesperson's share of speech will be too large and the customer will only listen.

That would not be good. The customer should also be involved in this phase and say something. There should also be an interactive conversation in this phase and not a monologue by the salesperson about his offer. Now there are very active customers who cannot be slowed down anyway and ask questions or raise critical objections even during the salesperson's presentation. With these, the strategy already explained during the needs assessment of working with counter-questions is good to use. For major objections during the presentation, these may need to be addressed in more detail. More on this shortly.

But then there are also those customers who are happy to let the salesperson talk over them, sit back, relax, and just listen. Especially when several people on the customer side take part in the conversation, it is often the case that one of them is the spokesperson. This does not have to be the main decision-maker. The other participants may only be listening silently, but they at least have a weighty say in the decision. Therefore, it is crucial to actively involve everyone and to achieve at least some interaction during the presentation as well.

Control questions in the presentation

The question type of choice for the situation just described are the confirmation or control questions. There are several ways to use these in your presentation.

On the one hand, it is important to clarify whether an argument or a product advantage is interesting for the customer:

- *"What do you think of that?"*
- *"How do you like that?"*
- *"Does this meet your needs?"*

Regularly attach such questions to product benefits you are presenting:

- Seller: *"The vehicle has six airbags. This ensures that you and your family are optimally protected in the event of a collision. And safety is particularly important to you, have I understood that correctly?"* Customer: *"Yes, exactly."*

In this way, you make the customer feel understood, pick up yeses, and get the customer - if you do this several times in a row - to switch into a kind of approval mode. This, in turn, is good for the conclusion, where the customer is supposed to say the final yes.

Of course, it could also be that the customer answers no. In that case, you have the important information that you may have misunderstood something and can correct this mistake.

Specifically, it is important to activate individual, reticent people (especially if several are present) and bring them into the conversation by addressing them directly:

- *"And you, Mr. Mayer, what do you think of it?" (Asked quite neutrally)*
- *"On a scale of 1 - 10, how do you like this feature?"* (control question combined with a scale question)
- *"How well do you like the ability to turn on your stove by cell phone?"* (Leading question, implying that it is well liked).
- Salesperson: *"Mrs. Müller, you are so taciturn, don't you like it?"* (Somewhat more provocative variant) Customer: *"No, no, I think it's good too."* The customer will often try to revise the passive impression she left by eagerly agreeing. Or she will become active and ask a question:
  "Mmmh, what I wanted to ask: Does this work at lower temperatures?"

Ecology issues in the presentation

Ecology questions go a bit further than control questions in the presentation phase. This means that you not only check the approval of individual points, benefit arguments, or features of your offer, but also ask what the effects will be and how compatible they will be for the customer and his environment.

On the one hand, this can serve to reinforce positive effects of points where there is hardly anything negative. In this way, the customer convinces himself of the attractiveness of these points or of your offer as a whole.

- Salesperson: *"If we put a counter-current system in the pool, how would that affect your daily life?"*
  Customer: *"Well, I'd use the pool much more often and finally have a real swim, which I've been meaning to do for a long time anyway."*

- Salesperson: *"What do you think different inserts and attachments do for you on this gas grill?"* (Leading question with the insinuation that the accessories have a positive effect).
  Customer: *"I certainly wouldn't get bored with it. I would grill more different things and probably my wife would grill more often."*

On the other hand, ecology questions can also reveal critical issues that the customer may not have thought of. Even if this doesn't sound desirable, it has advantages for customers and sellers. As already described in the first part, you thus avoid complaints, problems or even cancellations after the purchase, if the customer only then discovers the critical points in his practice.

- *"As discussed, we can offer the seminar outside of normal working hours. How will your employees react when they hear you are scheduled to sit in on the seminar on Saturday?"* (Circular ecology question)
- *"Your house would look like this with the facade in red. What would be the reaction of the neighbors? What do you think?"* (Hypothetical circular ecology question)
- *"If you wanted to find critical points about this model, what might they be?"* (If you want to look even harder for potential objections and dangers).

Objection handling

When dealing with objections, there is one cardinal mistake that is made extremely often: The salesperson immediately goes on the defense and tries to invalidate the objection with arguments. This can work if the argument is the very clear solution to the objection.

- Customer: *"I think the color is ugly."*
  Seller: *"No problem. You can choose your color from over 1,000 variants. There's sure to be something suitable."*

In this case, the customer is probably satisfied and the objection settled. But often, arguments as answers to objections are of little use or even make matters worse. The customer raises an objection and the salesperson responds with a counter-argument. The customer does not want to admit defeat yet and repeats his objection (sometimes in a slightly modified version), the salesman finds a counter-argument for it again. After a few rounds, both are buried so deeply in their positions that it is very difficult to get out again and return to a normal level of conversation.

- Customer: *"I don't like it."*
  Salesman: *"But this is the new fashion."*
  Customer: *"I still don't like it."*
  Seller: *"At the fashion shows in Paris last week, this is exactly the style that was presented."*
  Customer: *"That may be so. But I don't like it."*
  Seller: *"But it would look very good on you."* ... You see where this is going.

When the customer raises an objection, the primary goal is not to get it out of the way, but to understand it first. You achieve this by asking questions and, above all, listening very carefully.

To be more specific, a few examples of common objections that can be found in many industries:

- *"But that's expensive!"* (This is the No. 1 objection in very many industries).
- *"We already have a vendor for that."*
- *"It's too late for us."*
- *"I don't like it."*

- *"The quality is not good enough."*
- *"It's not a good fit for our purposes."*

We could go on with this list now, but you better create your own with the objections you hear every day in your sales practice. In most industries - including yours, presumably - you cover the topic with five to ten objections. You're unlikely to hear many more. But that also means you can prepare for every single objection you might hear. There aren't that many.

Even a short objection from a customer is multi-layered and multi-faceted in terms of how it is handled and resolved. You can divide the objection handling itself into several phases again. Questions play a decisive role in all of these phases.

The phases are:

1. Understand and concretize objections,
2. Challenge objections,
3. Solve objections.

Let's take a step-by-step look at what questions you can apply at each stage.

Understanding and concretizing objections

What is striking about objections - including those listed above - is that they are often brought up in a very unspecific and sweeping way. What do you really know when the customer says, *"I don't like that?"* Not much. And if you don't know much, you should ask questions to find out more.

The question type of choice for this are concretization questions:

- *"What do you mean by that?"* (The open-ended question you can and should almost always ask in connection with objections).
- *"What exactly do you mean by that?"*
- *"What do you mean by 'don't like'?"*
- *"What exactly don't you like about it?" - "And what else?" - (If necessary, also question several times until the customer's point of view is absolutely clear to you).*
- *"Is it the style you don't like, or the execution and quality?" (Alterntaive question)*

In this way, you not only gain information and understanding of the customer's point of view, but you might also notice that the customer meant something completely different with his objection than you understood. Misunderstandings of this kind are the rule rather than the exception.

- "That's too expensive for me!" can mean, for example, the customer ...
  - does not have so much money that he can afford the product.
  - would have the money, but does not want to spend it on it.
  - would buy this, but his wife, boss, client, etc. would not agree to this expense.

- could finance the purchase through the bank, but does not want to do so.
- would have the money and would spend it, but the product is not valuable enough in his eyes or the price-performance ratio is not right.
- would spend the money, has seen the same or something comparable elsewhere but cheaper.
- brings the objection as a pretext to hide the real objection with it, which may have nothing to do with money at all.

As you can see, a small and seemingly insignificant objection can hide a lot of underlying concerns or issues. And this objection may not be the only thing to consider; we still need to determine how much the customer considers "too expensive". Is it 5 percent, 10 percent, or 50 percent? This is something that needs to be explored and understood. Especially with price objections, it's important to have a good understanding or at least a sense of how far the customer's expectations are from your pricing reality. You can ask about that, too:

- *"How much too high is the price for you?"*
- *"Too expensive is very relative. What amount are we talking about?"*
- *"Just for guidance, what is the dimension of your asking price?"* (Deliberately worded softly so that it is easier for the customer to state his ideas).

If your customer doesn't want to be shown his cards at this point - and that can be good when it comes to price - but wants you as the salesperson to make a suggestion first, you can make it easier for him by giving coarser categories (a kind of scale question):

- *"Are we talking five percent, 10 percent or even more?"*
- *"Is your asking price 1,000 euros, 900 euros or even lower?"*

This way, you can assess the customer's objections much better. This is the basis for a successful solution to the objection.

Challenge objections

Questioning objections is, so to speak, the extension of contretemps. It is not quite easy to say where one ends and the other begins. In the end, though, it's not really important to define that boundary. Rather, it's about digging deeper and finding out two things in particular:

- Why is the objection important?
- How important is the objection really?

There is always a motive behind the customer's objection. In most cases, this is clearly recognizable and logical. But be careful: Often, the motive seems to be clear, but in reality, there is something completely different behind it. For example, in the above example with the price objection, you could assume that the customer brings this because he wants to save money when shopping. That could be the case. But the following motives could be behind it just as well:

- He is embarrassed that he does not have enough money.
- He doesn't want a fight with his wife or a reprimand from his boss for spending too much.
- He wants to feel that he has negotiated well and has not been taken advantage of.
- He wants to hide another objection and therefore pushes the price objection.

There are probably also other motives that we would possibly not even dream of. How do you find out about motives (not only in the case of objections, but in general)? Correct: by asking questions and, above all, by listening and looking very carefully. Even if why-questions have a bad image, they can be used in exactly the right way at this point - always assuming tact.

- *"Can I ask why this is important to you?"*
- *"Without wanting to be indiscreet, but this point seems to be very important to you. May I ask why?*
- *"So that I can better understand your motivations and find the appropriate solution for you, would you tell me why you are making this point?"*

Suppose you combine the why question with a permission to ask and/or a rationale for your question, as in these examples. In that case, the likelihood that your interviewer will give you deeper insights increases significantly.

The second important point in this phase is to determine how important the objection or its solution is to the customer. It can be a very weak objection (a small, delicate request) or a massive one, a knockout criterion. Of course, with some objections, you can also tell how important this point is by the way it is formulated (as shown earlier in the book).

If this is not the case, you can also ask about the importance of the objection to the customer:

- *"How important is this issue to you?"*
- *"How important is it to you that we find a solution to this issue?"*
- *"On a scale of 1 (would be nice) to 10 (is a must), where do you rank this request?"* (The scale question helps the customer to be more specific).

But you can also get off the defensive at this point and use the objection to take a big step toward closure in the conversation by asking something like the following:

- *"Is there anything else keeping you from choosing our offer?"*

Your customer now has two options: Yes or No. If he answers yes in this case, then, of course, it's a matter of finding out what the other points are that are still preventing him from buying.

- *"I see. So what is it that's still on your mind?"*

In this way, you learn about further points or objections that - for whatever reason - have not yet been raised. If the customer answers no, then you have a conditional deal. This means that if you can resolve this objection to mutual satisfaction, the customer will buy.

At the same time, this question also has other positive effects on you:

- The customer must "come out" and put all his points, issues, and demands on the table. Some customers (sometimes professional buyers) use salami tactics. They negotiate on one point and when they have reached a solution there, they negotiate on the next one. In this way, they cut off more and more of your earnings, slice by slice (salami tactics, because they are often very thin slices). You tend to prevent that with this question.
- By asking questions this way, you are also signaling that you are serious and don't just sit down for coffee, but want the customer to buy from you.

What's interesting is that, in this case, even saying no in response to your question brings you a nice bit closer to closing the deal. So it doesn't always have to be the yes that leads to success. We will come to closing questions a little further on in the book.

The final and hardest question you can ask about the importance of the objection to the customer is the knockout question:

- *"Does that mean if we can't come to an agreement at this point,* ***you're not buying under any circumstances****?"*

- *"Does that mean that's an **absolute knockout criterion** for you?"*
- *"**Surely** the product is **out of the question for** you if we can't offer an alternative here?"*

By all means exaggerate the wording a little (see bold words in the questions). This strengthens the effect of this type of question. The customer will find it more difficult to say clearly that he would not buy something under any circumstances than that it is only an important purchase criterion for him. If he doesn't give you a clear rejection, then he leaves the door open for you a little longer and you can continue asking:

- Salesperson: *"So that means you'd like another alternative, but you'd also be happy with the current one?"*
  Customer: *"Yes, you could put it that way."*

This means that you do not yet have an order, but you are in a somewhat better and safer position than if you had not asked this question in all its clarity.

And if the customer gives as an answer that his point is a real knockout criterion? Then it is also good for you to know that. Either you don't have a solution, then you can stop the process here and save time with this customer, which you can use well for the next one. Or you find a solution, in which case it's all the better if you can solve such an extremely important issue.

Even if these questions sound tough and take a little more courage to ask, in the end you as a salesperson can only win with them.

(Resolve) objections

Now, when it comes to solving an objection, let us say in advance that it is a misconception that objections must always be solved. How often have you yourself bought something despite an objection, sometimes perhaps even a massive one? Actually, it was way too expensive for you and you bought it anyway - because other factors compensated for the higher price. If you're like me, you've even bought clothes or shoes (I have, several times) that actually didn't/do not fit and were hardly ever or never worn. Why? Because the beautiful piece looked so great and did not fit me, but it still fit me.

Assume that your customers may feel exactly the same way with regard to objections. Everything we buy has pros and cons, and we buy despite the cons if the pros outweigh the cons.

Sometimes, therefore, it can be absolutely sufficient to simply ignore the objection. With a little luck, especially if it's a weak objection, it won't come back.

If you want to do something more, questions are the communication technique of choice to resolve objections or have the customer resolve them.

Wordless questions

If the customer brings up an objection and you just look at them questioningly, that can be enough to resolve the objection.

- Customer: *"But the delivery time is already long."* Salesperson looks at customer questioningly. Customer: *"But I'll have a great new car for that."*

In this type of objection handling, the customer often begins to give himself the answers that the buyer would have given in order to outweigh the disadvantages of the objection and invalidate it. And, of course, if he says it himself, it carries more weight than any argument the seller might make.

Play back objection

This basic concept is also what runs through when it comes to the use of questions in solving objections: play the objection back to the customer by means of a question and let him solve the objection himself or at least contribute to the solution. We have already discussed this concept as a counter question in the first part of the book.

You can do this - depending on the situation - with a wide variety of questions:

- *"And what can we do about that?"*
- *"How do you think we can solve this?"*
- *"And what can I do there that would satisfy you enough to get you to order?"* (If you want to go directly toward closing.)
- *"If I offered you that we would also do the installation, would you choose us?"* (Hypothetical proposal question with conclusion orientation)

- *"If you were in my position, how would you respond to your concerns?"* (Hypothetical, circular question)
- *"You wanted to have this appointment with me yes, even though you knew the offer. Obviously there is something you like about it that outweighs your concerns. What is that?"* (A somewhat paradoxical question that you can use to counterattack).
- *"Given the many benefits, how easy would it be for you to live with this point?"* (Hypothetical suggestive question)

Of course, if you leave a lot of possible solutions open to the customer with a question such as *"What do you suggest?", which is* a possible course of action, they may seize the opportunity and ask for a solution that would remove the objection but is out of the question for you because, for example, the effort is too great.

In that case, you can tighten the scope a bit in advance or in a second round of questions to get - for you - more realistic suggestions.

- *"When it comes to price, my hands are absolutely tied. What else can I do to fulfill your wishes besides a discount?"*
- *"Right away, the delivery time is non-negotiable. So how can we solve this point?"*
- *"If we rule out color change, what else might satisfy you?"* (Hypothetical question)

This approach, as with all questions, has the added benefit of allowing the salesperson to maintain or regain control of the conversation.

Specialty price negotiation

In many industries, price objections are the ones that occur most often and are also the most annoying and difficult for many salespeople to deal with. I have already brought some examples of these and how you can deal with them in the last few paragraphs. But dealing with price objections is such a broad area with an extremely large number of possibilities for the salesperson that it would go beyond the scope of this book.

That's why I wrote another book about this: "Price Objection Handling Made Easy". You can get it at this link > https://amzn.to/3kwwSUj

Conclusion

Closing questions are among the classic questions in sales. Closing the sale is often regarded as a high art, and it is such an important phase in sales that there are many books on the subject, as well as seminars on closing techniques. And yes, the closing is, of course, important. It is the closing of the sale that actually turns the prospect into a customer. Without closing, there is no business.

From an overarching perspective, closing the deal is not all that special. It is simply the logical consequence of what has previously been initiated and implemented by the salesperson in a good sales talk or a professional sales process.

In the end, the only thing that matters in the closing process is to "push" the customer (sometimes more forcefully) to get him to decide to buy. Of course, there are those customers who don't need to be pushed, but who say yes faster than the salesperson could push them and head for the cash register with their booty - metaphorically speaking.

However, in sales practice - perhaps in yours as well - there are also a significant number of customers who do not find it easy to make up their minds. The reasons for this can be manifold, such as:

- You are not yet (quite) sure if it would be the right decision.
- You still want or need to get approval from someone else - the boss or the partner.
- You don't have the money to do it (yet) and may still need to line up the funding.

- They just want to "sleep on it" because they have made it a rule to do so before making a major decision.
- You are still waiting for more offers from your competitors.
- They are playing coy for tactical reasons, perhaps to elicit concessions from you.

But for whatever reason, the customer has not yet said yes, it makes sense to motivate him to make a decision and trigger it. Either new, as yet unknown objections emerge as a result - in which case you can deal with them as I described in the previous chapter. Or the customer takes heart and decides in favor of your offer. In both cases, you will move forward.

And this "pushing" (and I use this word quite deliberately to indicate that it must be done with tact) happens, in keeping with the theme of this book, naturally with questions. In addition to these, two other factors are needed, especially in the closing, to bring the sale to a good conclusion. One is a portion of courage to ask the decisive question. The other essential element is the persistent silence after the question, to really wait for the customer's answer.

Courage is needed because if the customer could say no - then everything would have been for nothing. After all the effort of a sales process and the hopeful prospect of a great order, a no is naturally painful. And yet, at this point, an open no is better than one that isn't said but is there nonetheless. You know the cases where you run after the customer for what feels like an eternity without getting a decision, and then you can no longer reach him at some point. I prefer a clear no. Then I can either do something to make it a yes (by dealing with the objections behind it), or I have time to devote myself to the next customer.

For the closing questions themselves, another distinction can be made that we have not yet made for the question types. It makes sense to divide closing questions into the following two categories:

- direct closing questions and
- indirect closing questions.

Direct completion questions, as the name implies, ask directly about completion:

- *"Do you want to buy the product?"*
- *"Are you sticking with this variant?"*
- *"Can I release the order?"*
- *"Do you take version A or version B?"* (Also possible as an alternative question.)

The indirect closing questions work somewhat differently. Instead of directly asking for the customer's agreement to the offer, they come through the back door. Most of the time, they are leading questions that include the conclusion as a pre-assumption.

- *"When do you want us to deliver?"*
- *"How do you want to pay? Cash or card?"* (Indirect Alternative Question)
- *"What else, besides the bike itself, do you need?"*
- *"Would you like us to set it up, too?"*

When the customer responds to such questions, he already agrees to the purchase. Whether this agreement is clear enough and a yes to the purchase can be concluded from it depends on the respective situation and how communication has proceeded up to this point. A clear *"Yes, I want to have that",* as is usual with direct closing questions, will often no longer be the case with indirect ones.

The no as a yes

Even with direct closing questions, the customer does not always have to answer yes or agree in order for you to receive an order. Even a no can get you the deal you've been longing for. How do you do it? All you have to do is ask the following question, which you already know from dealing with objections:

- *"Is there anything else keeping you from choosing our offer?"*

If the customer now answers no, you have a deal. In my experience, this type of question - which could also be counted among the indirect ones - often requires less courage from the salesperson and passes more easily from his lips. But it is also sometimes easier for customers to say no than yes.

Silence after the final question

As mentioned at the beginning of this chapter, silence after questions is a very crucial element - and especially after closing questions. Silence is still relatively easy for salespeople when asking questions in the context of needs assessment, for example. After all, a question is asked in order to obtain information from the customer. Therefore, they wait for the answer more or less patiently.

It's different with closing questions. Here, the nervous tension of the salesperson is usually much higher than in the relaxed phase of the needs analysis. This is especially the case when the deal is more important or involves higher sales.

What I then often observe with salespeople is that after the closing question - instead of remaining silent - they continue talking and "chattering up" the deal, as this behavior is often referred to.

- *"Do you want to book this trip? ... It is really ideal for your needs. The hotel is perfect and also the options you ..."*

After the question mark, this salesperson should be quiet and wait for the customer's answer - a yes or a no in this case. If it should be a no, then two steps back into objection handling - with questions, of course.

Instead, in this example, the salesperson voluntarily goes back into the presentation and begins to argue why this journey is so ideal for the customer. That's not even necessary at this point. That's already been done. Now it's just a matter of getting the customer's yes.

The question is: Why does this happen relatively often? Because of fear of the No. If the customer is given room for an answer here, then it could ultimately be No. And to avoid this, the salesperson does not give the customer this room. And to avoid that, the salesperson doesn't give the customer that space. He texts him. Yet a clear no - as discussed in a previous section - is something that you, as a salesperson, can definitely do something with.

Upselling

What does upselling mean? Based on a wish, a need, or even a decision already made by the customer in favor of an offer, upselling is the introduction of a higher-value and, thus, normally also higher-priced offer. In the case of a car, classic upsell offers include the 250-horsepower variant rather than the 190-horsepower variant, leather upholstery rather than fabric upholstery on the seats, the sports package rather than the basic equipment, and so on. These kinds of higher-value products or performance variants exist in many areas.

Basically, upselling is about whetting the customer's appetite for something better, more beautiful, more expensive, and awakening the need for it or making it stronger. Here, too, you can of course work very well with questions.

- *"Have you ever thought about the beautiful Nappa leather trim on the seats?*
- *"What - perhaps secret - other wishes do you have in relation to this product?"*
- *"So what do you think of the deluxe version?"*
- *"How do you like this slightly larger product?"*
- *"Do you want the VIP seats in the front rows?"* (Right away in the form of a direct closing question)

Questions that are suitable for upselling can also be found in the needs assessment and in the closing. It all depends on where you start with the upsell. It is often more clever than offering the customer the better version too directly to bring it into play more indirectly through questions.

- *"Have you heard that Brad Pitt (or a celebrity of your choice) also regularly stays there?"*
- *"Did you know that the majority of our customers reach for the Platinum package?"*
- *"Could you imagine spending your vacation in a suite instead of a double room?"*

This allows you to anchor the idea or even the image of it in the customer's mind and make it work there.

Attention paternalism

However, the most important thing in upselling is not the type of questions you use for it but that you think about the upsell at all. Many salespeople are satisfied with the fact that the customer buys the basic version. Along the lines of "I'd rather have a bird in the hand than a pigeon on the rooftop." After all, the pigeon might get away while trying to catch it.

Often it is also a misconceived consideration of the customer's wallet or budget. The customer is not expected to pay the more expensive upsell. From the seller's point of view, the additional benefit may not be worth the extra price. But the salesperson's view is only the salesperson's view and has nothing to do with the customer's view - or at least should have nothing to do with it. Patronizing the customer in this way and not offering him the best you have to offer in the first place could also be described as arrogant and patronizing.

Therefore, the motto is: Make sure you give the customer the best you have for him and let him decide for himself whether he wants it. And yes, do it with tact.

Cross-selling /additional-sales

Cross-selling is a close relative of upselling. Cross-selling is also about making more sales with one and the same customer and thus better exploiting existing customer potential. The German terms "Zusatzverkauf" or "cross-selling" aptly describe what it is all about. Instead of selling a higher-value and higher-priced version of the main product or a larger quantity of something, as in upselling, cross-selling is about selling things that complement and complete the main product or core service. These can be, for example:

- the bag to the camera,
- the trip to the vacation trip,
- the warranty extension to the washing machine,
- the coffee after dinner.

These are classic examples of cross-selling offers. Done correctly, cross-selling not only generates more sales for the seller, but also brings additional benefits for the customer. He benefits significantly more from his purchase as a result.

Imagine you are buying a flashlight and the seller is not doing a good job of the add-on sale. When you go to put it into operation, you realize that you clearly need batteries, but you don't have any. You are justifiably upset. Perhaps at not having thought of it yourself, but also at the salesman, whose job it would have been to remind you.

In many areas, cross-selling is not a particularly difficult matter either. Often, these are additional offers that the customer would be very happy to buy if they were reminded of them. And this reminder can be done very well - how could it be otherwise - in the form of questions. The basic attitude you should have towards additional offers is that the question is not whether the customer needs or wants something additional, but only WHAT and HOW MUCH of it.

- *"What more do you need?"*
- *"Do you have enough coals left at home?"*
- *"Is the six-pack enough for you, or would you rather go with the 12-pack to avoid running out during operation?"*
- *"How do you put the device into operation?"* (For the additional sale of service)
- *"What about your staffing capabilities in terms of commissioning?"*
- *"Have you heard anything about XY (product)?"*
    - *"No." >> "Can I tell you about it?"*
    - *"Yes." >> "And what?"*
- *"Did you know that you can also use XY (product) in combination with AB (product)?"*
- *"Did you know that most of the problems in the operation of this product are due to poor installation and commissioning?"*
- *"How regularly do you manage to inspect the facility to the recommended (required) standards?"*

- *"If you could wish for one more thing in relation to the seminar for your employees, what would it be?"* (Hypothetical variant)
- *"What do you miss about your current solution?"*
- *"What caused the most problems using the product in the past?"*
- *"Do you like to eat sweets?"*

Of course, especially in additional selling, it is very easy to work with suggestive questions. As the questioning professional you are by now, you will have noticed that some of the above questions are at least slightly suggestive and involve presuppositions. But this works much better with the following questions:

- *"What dessert do you want?"* (Open suggestive question)
- *"Would you rather have the apple pie or the vanilla ice cream for dessert?"* (Alternative leading question)
- *"With the current temperatures, like most of our guests, do you prefer our famous apple pie or would you prefer a light, cool sorbet?"* (Alternative suggestive question with a few amplifiers)

As you can see from some of these questions, the transitions between upselling and cross-selling are often fluid. However, it is not necessary or possible to draw a precise dividing line between the two sales strategies since both usually happen in one and the same sales conversation.

Basically, you do a small additional needs assessment for the additional sale after the customer has decided on the main product. Of course, right from the start, you collect information that indicates the potential for additional products or services, and you also hint here and there that there are other options and possibilities. But the actual add-on selling should really be done after the customer has decided on the main product; otherwise, it may confuse or distract the customer too much and delay or prevent the purchase decision. First things first.

Complaints and grievances

As the last of the sales situations, we now come to the handling of complaints. By their very nature, these can only take place after the customer has already purchased. Basically, it is an objection after the purchase. Therefore, much of what you read in the chapter on handling objections also applies here. Therefore, I won't repeat that here, but I will only address one specific aspect of this situation.

What makes the complaint situation so special and often so unpleasant for salespeople is the fact that the customer is often very emotional in the process. He is annoyed, angry, frustrated or even aggressive. This makes communication with him very difficult. In order to be able to talk to the customer reasonably and find a common solution, you first have to de-escalate the situation and reduce the negative emotions. And this can be done very well with the right questions.

Often, when dealing with highly emotional customers, salespeople make the mistake of trying to calm them down. The customer is loud, perhaps even speaking in an aggressive tone. If the salesperson now says with a friendly smile, *"Now, calm down first. That's not so bad already.",* then this can lead to the fact that the customer explodes now only so correctly. This is understandable because, with his statement and his way of speaking, the salesperson is signaling to the customer that he has not understood him and probably has not listened properly - but in the worst case, he is also signaling that he does not really take the customer's current concern seriously. If he did, he would not remain so calm in the face of such a catastrophe. The customer may therefore repeat his complaint even louder to finally make the salesperson understand that this is a serious and important matter. You see where this leads.

The better way to deal with such a customer in such a situation is to first get down to his emotional level in order to be able to understand the anger, frustration and uncertainty. This should also show in your body language. This makes you more like the customer and thus more likeable, a little bit at least. This creates a common basis from which you can now continue to work and steer the conversation or the customer in the right direction. This emotional pickup is illustrated by this graphic.

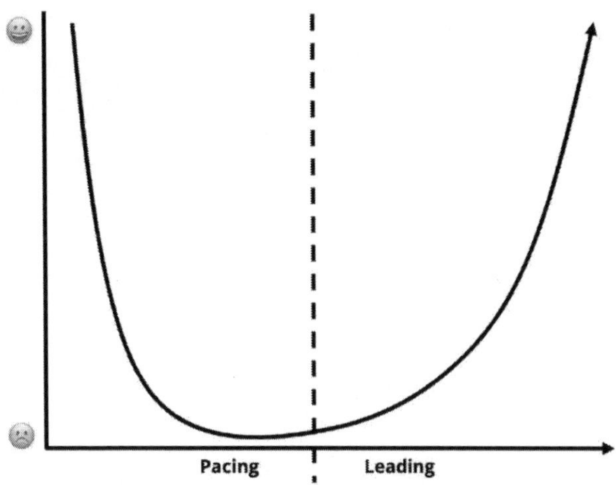

In the first phase, "Adapt and pick up" (also called pacing), you approach the customer emotionally and pick him up where he is. In doing so, you signal to him, *"I understand you and your concern is important to me."* You do or show this by approximating your voice, tone of voice, words used and body language to what the customer is showing. This means you also need to sound and appear somewhat agitated, annoyed, concerned, or frustrated - depending on what emotion your customer is in. And for most salespeople, that goes against the automatic reaction of wanting to appear reassuring.

In the second phase (Leading), you then steer the conversation in the direction of problem-solving. Now that you have sufficiently understood and picked up the customer, you can take the lead. Here you then change your body language and voice step by step and thus also the emotions that you show and also feel yourself in the direction of relaxation.

Complaints are often - because very emotional - also very imprecise and unspecific. *"That's an impertinence! That doesn't work like that! That doesn't work!"* Based on such statements, you as a salesperson cannot yet understand what the customer means.

"First understand, then be understood."

You must first understand the customer, and then be understood by him, and to this end you must ask questions.

Questions for the "Fit and Pick Up" phase

In the first phase, the questions are about showing understanding, but at the same time gathering information to create a basis for problem solving.

- *"What happened?"*
- *"What exactly happened?" (Question for concretization, if the customer raises the complaint in a very unspecific way).*
- *"When exactly was that?"*
- *"How exactly did that go down?"*
- *"What got you so upset?"*
- *"What's the problem?"*

The concretization questions gently force the customer to switch from the emotional lane to the factual one. It is an impossibility to keep the anger or frustration at a high level for a long time when answering such questions.

With a simple question like *"What happened?"* (still without any specifics), you will prompt the customer to repeat his complaint. Very often, you will notice that even with one repetition, the emotionality decreases. Time is also a factor that helps you in this.

As the conversation progresses, the time factor alone will lower the emotional waves. Hardly anyone can get worked up about a complaint over a long period of time. Think about something you complained about a few days, weeks, or months ago. Very often, it has become so unimportant that you even have a hard time remembering it.

Be careful at this stage with emotion-related questions such as *"How do you feel about this now?"* These have the effect of amplifying emotions. Therefore, you should only use them if you want to achieve exactly that - to escalate further before de-escalating. However, this is an approach that should only be used in very specific cases. The customer would be emotionally "exhausted" by this approach and thus clear his head for more objectivity.

Even though this book is primarily about questions, it should be noted at this point that it is very beneficial to express one's own understanding or even compassion by making appropriate statements, especially at the beginning of a complaint situation or a complaint conversation (and also between questions).

- *"I can relate to that."*
- *"That you're upset there, I understand perfectly."*
- *"If that happened to me, I'd be frustrated, too."*

Since this phase is very much about establishing a good relationship level with the customer, the "active listening" described at the beginning is the conversation technique that is particularly important in addition to good questions.

Studies in department store complaints departments have shown that compassion and empathy are the key success factors in dealing with complaints. Complaining customers who were given an extreme amount of understanding but little money felt significantly better treated than those who were shown financial generosity but not emotional generosity.

Questions for the "Take the lead" phase

Then, when the relationship level is sustainable and the initial emotionality has been reduced to a level where you can talk reasonably with your customer and look for solutions, you can take the lead. The best way to do this is to ask questions again because *"He who asks, leads!"* as we have already established.

You can ask for possible solutions from the customer with open questions:

- *"What do you suggest?"*
- *"What solution do you have in mind?"*
- *"What course of action would make you happy?"*

However, you should only ask this type of question if you are willing and able to implement the customer's suggestions or wishes. If you assume that the customer would propose solutions that are inappropriate and would cost you too much, you should not ask too open questions, but proceed differently.

You could work with closed questions at this point:

- *"Should we exchange the product?"*
- *"Do you want your money back?"*
- *"Should we repair the damage?"*

While this way of asking is fine, there are a few other, more communicatively adept questioning techniques you can use here. Alternative questions, for example:

- "Should we repair the product or better exchange it?"
- "Do you want your money back or a gift certificate that you can then use to choose something else from our selection?"

Alternative questions have the advantage here that the customer can choose, even if it is you who controls the result by specifying the choice. You control the result even more if you use suggestive questions:

- *"Do you want to leave it right here so we can fix it?"* (A thoroughly cleverly suggestive question, implying that repair as a solution to the problem is okay with the customer).

- *"When do you have time to bring the unit in for repair?"* (This takes it a step further by assuming not only that repair is acceptable as a solution, but also that the customer will bring the product to you).

- *"Do you want to just keep using the product and we'll give you a voucher worth 10 euros as an apology for the problems you had, or would you rather we repair it?"* (An alternative question that excludes, for example, the possibility of an exchange or a reversal).

The formulation as a suggestion question (although suggestions are also built into the questions in the previous variants) can also be used very well at this point:

- *"What do you say we send someone over right away to take a look at the problem on site?"* (This also allows you to use open-ended questions without running the risk of being confronted with excessive demands from the customer).
- ***"Most of our customers** want to continue using the product in such a case and are **happy to** take a 100-euro voucher as a consolation gift. What do you think of this solution?"* (An open proposal question with a strongly suggestive component. It is prefaced as a fact that this solution is fine for most customers and is **gladly** accepted).

The type of questioning you use to lead the complaint case to a happy ending for both sides ultimately depends very much on the solution options you have or want to use. However you go about it, make a strategy for it and define a standard process for yourself that also includes the appropriate questions.

THE NEXT STEPS

We have almost reached the end of this book. You may have read it normally, from cover to cover, or - especially in the second part - you may have gone straight to the sections that concern you and your daily practice and are of particular interest to you. However you proceeded, you were hopefully able to take one or the other question from it and ideally already apply it successfully. Congratulations!

To make sure that this is exactly what happens more often, it is important to work on it. The real implementation work starts only now after you have read the book. The reading itself was more like the warm-up phase. If I could convince you that questions are a very helpful tool in many of your sales situations to close them even more successfully or even faster, then I now recommend the following:

Create question lists for your practice

For each sales situation (needs assessment, objection handling, closing, etc.) that is relevant in your practice, create a list of specific questions. In some situations, two or three really good ones may be enough for you (for example, in closing the sale). In other situations, such as needs assessment, the list will be somewhat longer or even - depending on the industry and the offer - very long.

The questions from this book can serve you as a basis, as an idea, but in many cases, they will not fit exactly (which would also be an impossibility). Make your own list that is perfectly suited to your needs. You can and should expand it over time, as you will always come up with more supplementary questions in practical use. Some you will also cross off the list again in the process. The effort to create these lists is not very big. It will be quite easy for you.

Work with question lists in sales

You should always have these question lists with you in sales. In some cases, you can work with them directly and visibly for the customer. In most cases, for example, there is nothing to be said against working through the questions together with the customer in the form of a checklist when assessing requirements. Especially not when it comes to more complex solutions, larger investments, or products and services that require intensive consulting. Quite the opposite, in fact. It makes you look very professional and well-prepared to the customer. For you as a salesperson, it's an easy way to make sure you don't forget anything.

If you have mainly telephone customer contact, then using your question list is even easier. You can have it lying at your workplace so that you can take a look at it at any time.

For some situations in sales, working directly with question lists is not appropriate or possible. For example, it would look very strange if you were to read off the closing question from your list. In these cases, I recommend that you have the question lists with you and take a look at them every now and then - ideally immediately before customer meetings so that you have them fresh in your mind. Besides, it's a good opportunity to use any waiting times productively.

However you use the question lists, they will become so much second nature to you over time that you will fall into question mode quite automatically in various situations. And that is exactly the goal. Only when you ask questions without having to focus specifically on them do you have the opportunity to turn your attention fully back to the customer, their answers and their behavior. And that's where all your attention should ultimately be.

QUESTIONS AS A PANACEA

Now we are at the end of a book full of questions, which has asked many questions, answered many, and probably raised a few new ones and left them unanswered. You may have gotten the impression that questions are the panacea for all communication challenges in sales and customer contact. They aren't. Of course, there are plenty of other tools, tactics, and approaches whose use will move you forward significantly in your customer conversations. But since the book is one that has made questioning techniques and their use in sales its theme, I have briefly touched on other useful tools on one or two appropriate occasions, but have not gone into depth.

Since it's always difficult to say what's more important and what's less important when it comes to these kinds of topics, and since my nature is much more inclined to shades of gray than to black-and-white views, I wouldn't claim that questions are the most important communication tool in sales. However, I would be tempted to claim that they are among the most important tools you should really master in customer contact. And even though this book is about sales, I'd argue that it's also true for many, if not all, areas of life. After all, selling is not limited to the business world alone. Aren't we selling something all the time?

Have fun selling and good luck with it.

Best regards,

ABOUT THE AUTHOR

Marketing and pricing expert Roman Kmenta has been active internationally for more than 30 years as an entrepreneur, keynote speaker and bestselling author. The business economist and serial entrepreneur provides his many years of international marketing and sales experience in both the B2B and B2C sectors today to over 100 top companies as well as many small businesses and sole proprietors in Germany, Switzerland and Austria.

More than 25,000 people read his blog or listen to his podcast every week. With his talks, he provides thought-provoking impulses for salespeople, executives and entrepreneurs on the topic of "profitable growth" and sets impulses for his listeners and readers in the direction of a value-oriented sales and marketing approach.

www.romankmenta.com

Photo: Matern, Vienna

Perfect for international sales organizations

1 book in 23 languages

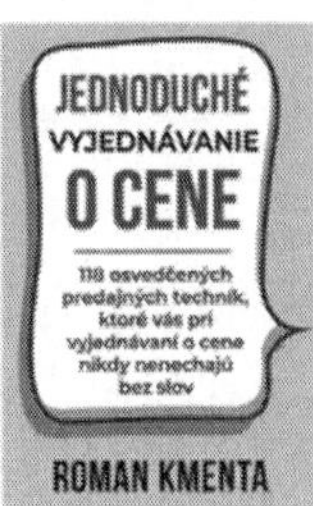

For more information:

https://www.romankmenta.com/buch-zu-teuer-international

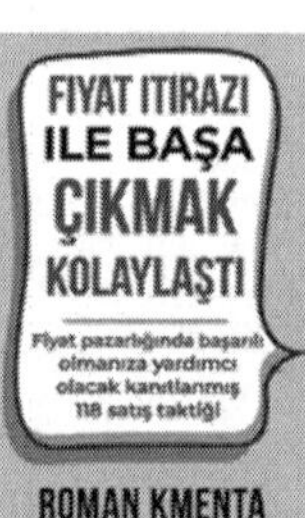

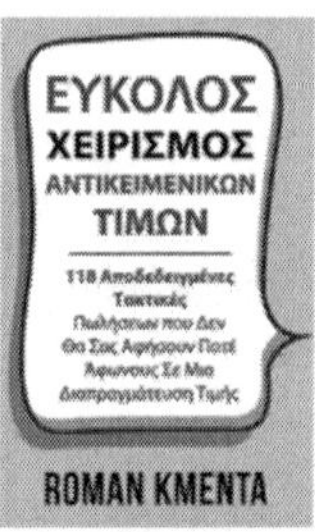

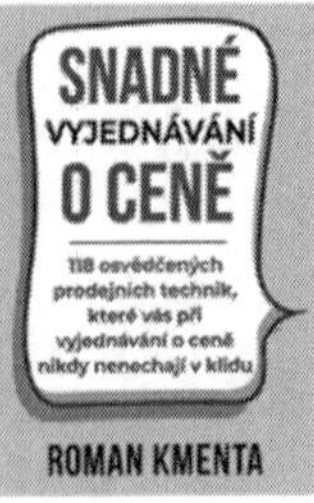

ROMAN KMENTA
CHARGE
MORE
EARN
MORE
How to
confidently
increase prices
without losing
customers
A practical sales guide
for managers, entrepreneurs
and salespeople.
BUSINESS IN A
NUTSHEL
Practical knowledge
in a compact form.

Charge more earn more

Top strategies to enforce higher prices!

Achieving higher prices is a key success factor for most companies. A very special challenge is to carry out price increases with existing customers in such a way that the customer remains a customer. It is important to know about and implement a number of decisive strategies in sales and marketing.

This book is dedicated to these strategies. Pricing and price increases are issues that affect the entire company. Roman Kmenta 84 Accordingly, some of the recommended approaches are comprehensive, far-reaching, and in-depth. At the same time, you will also find tips in this book that can be implemented quickly and easily, which will make the next price increase easier and bring you a lot of money.

In this book, you will learn:

- when the optimal time is for a price increase
- how not to make a price increase look like one
- how to avoid price comparability
- how to increase the value of your offer in the eyes of the customer
- how to avoid price negotiations
- which price psychological affects you should be aware of
- which arguments you can use to support a price increase
- how to raise prices without raising prices.

Higher prices, higher contribution margins, and more income.

A book that pays off.

https://amzn.to/3FwTV7q

ROMAN KMENTA
HOW TO
WRITE OFFERS
THAT SELL
44
psychological
strategies to create
a successful offer
A practical sales guide for
managers, entrepreneurs
and salespeople
BUSINESS IN A
NUTSHEL
Practical knowledge
in a compact form.

How to write offers that sell

44 psychological strategies to create a successful offer!

Written offers are a greatly underestimated instrument in the sales process. A lot of companies produce many of them, but pay little attention to them. Offers are silent salespeople, who spend more time with or at the customer, than the sales force in some business areas and industries.

So how can you raise the potential that lurks in your offers and turn them into better sellers? How can you design your offers to convince your customers?

In this book you will learn

- why your customers basically don't care about your offer and what they are really interested in
- how to build up offers effectively in terms of sales psychology
- how your offers can be made much more attractive with the right design
- what the most promising ways of delivering your offers are
- which price psychological strategies you use to make your offers appear more favorable
- how you clearly differentiate yourself from your competitors through your offers
- what a "Shock and Awe Package" is and how you can use it in a targeted manner.

Better offers bring more sales to a close.

A book that pays off.

https://amzn.to/3spYjA6

Made in the USA
Middletown, DE
02 January 2025